DEVIL'S ADVOCATES

DEVIL'S ADVOCATES is a series of books devoted to exploring the classics of horror cinema. Contributors to the series come from the fields of teaching, academia, journalism and fiction, but all have one thing in common: a passion for the horror film and a desire to share it with the widest possible audience.

'The admirable Devil's Advocates series is not only essential – and fun – reading for the serious horror fan but should be set texts on any genre course.'
Dr Ian Hunter, Reader in Film Studies, De Montfort University, Leicester

'Auteur Publishing's new Devil's Advocates critiques on individual titles... offer bracingly fresh perspectives from passionate writers. The series will perfectly complement the BFI archive volumes.' **Christopher Fowler, *Independent on Sunday***

'Devil's Advocates has proven itself more than capable of producing impassioned, intelligent analyses of genre cinema... quickly becoming the go-to guys for intelligent, easily digestible film criticism.' ***Horror Talk.com***

'Auteur Publishing continue the good work of giving serious critical attention to significant horror films.' ***Black Static***

 DevilsAdvocatesbooks

DevilsAdBooks

DEVIL'S ADVOCATES

PEEPING TOM

KIRI BLOOM WALDEN

ACKNOWLEDGEMENTS

I could not have written the book without Thelma Schoonmaker's help – she really helped me to understand how Michael Powell felt about *Peeping Tom*, and the impact it had on his career. Talking to Thelma, and to Columba Powell, was the closest I could get to talking to Powell himself.

The film itself could easily have been lost forever if Martin Scorsese had not saved it when he did. Along with Ian Christie in the UK and Bertrand Tavernier in France (among others), Scorsese's promotion of *Peeping Tom* has enabled the film to be reappraised and appreciated.

Thank you also to two helpful readers, Ian Bird and Rob Daniel, and to Steve Crook, whose website www.powell-pressburger.org has been invaluable.

The author went through a car crash, the birth of a baby, and Covid-19 lockdown in the course of writing this book, so the final thank you is reserved for the ever-patient Sam Walden.

First published in 2020 by
Auteur, an imprint of
Liverpool University Press,
4 Cambridge Street,
Liverpool
L69 7ZU

Series design: Nikki Hamlett at Cassels Design
Set by Cassels Design www.casselsdesign.co.uk
Printed and bound by CPI Group (UK) Ltd, Croydon CR0 4YY

British Library Cataloguing-in-Publication Data
A catalogue record for this book is available from the British Library

ISBN paperback: 978-1-80034-807-3
ISBN hardback 978-1-80034-837-0
ISBN epub: 978-1-80034-773-1
ISBN PDF: 978-1-80034-606-2

CONTENTS

PLOT SUMMARY

Mark Lewis is a young man living in London who works as a film camera focus puller at a film studio. He lives in a large house, his childhood home, which is now subdivided into flats. He lives in one flat and rents the others out.

The film begins with the murder of a prostitute. We witness the murder through the lens of the camera being held by the unidentified killer. Mark is revealed as the killer only when we see him in his flat, watching back the film of the murder he has committed.

Mark also works part time as a porn photographer, in a studio above a newsagent shop. We see Mark overcome with fascination when he is asked to photograph a facially scarred model.

Back at Mark's house, a young woman, Helen Stephens, is celebrating her 21st birthday. Helen shares one of the flats in Mark's house with her blind, alcoholic mother. Helen sees Mark and invites him in, but he shyly declines. Instead Helen comes up to his flat with a slice of birthday cake. Mark shows her films that his deceased father, a scientist, shot of his experiments with Mark as a boy. His father's research was into fear, and the films show Mark's father deliberately frightening and upsetting his young son.

At the film studio where he works, Mark is friendly with an aspiring actress, Viv. She agrees to meet Mark after hours to shoot a showreel, thinking that the filming will enable her to get more work. But when they meet in the empty studio Mark explains to Viv that the film is for his own project, a film about fear. We see him reveal that his tripod has a knife attachment. Mark advances towards Viv and we see through his camera that he is killing her. Her body falls into a prop trunk.

Later that evening Mark and Helen meet again. They get on well, he gives her a brooch as a birthday present and she tells him about a children's book she is writing, about a magic camera.

Mrs Stephens, Helen's mother, is suspicious of Mark. When Helen and Mark return home after a dinner date Mark goes into his flat and discovers Mrs Stephens in his screening room. She suspects Mark may have committed a crime and questions him. He watches back his latest attempt to capture the fear of death on film. With the sound turned off, Mrs Stephens has no idea of the content of the films being projected. For a moment, it looks like Mark might kill Mrs Stephens, but as she is blind he does not, because unlike the other victims she is incapable of anticipating her imminent death.

Back in the studio, Viv's body is discovered. When the police arrive Mark films them. The police have called in a psychiatrist to advise on the possible psychological characteristics and motivation of the murderer. Mark tells the psychiatrist of his own father's work and asks about scopophilia (voyeurism). This leads one police detective to be suspicious of Mark.

Mark goes back to the porn photography studio over the shop. He kills Milly, one of the models, and leaves, this time observed by the police officer who is following him.

While Mark is out, Helen has gone to Mark's room and has seen the film which shows a victim dying. Mark returns while she is still in his flat. He explains his attempts to capture fear – the moment of death, on camera. He shows her how he did it, with a knife mounted on his camera tripod and a mirror attached to the front, so the murder victim witnesses their own death.

As the police arrive at his home, Mark triggers cameras to record his own death then commits suicide using the tripod knife he has previously murdered his victims with. Helen falls to the floor crying as the police come in.

Chapter 1: *Peeping Tom* in 1960

Peeping Tom is a low budget British film released in 1960 that had a profoundly negative impact on the career of its director Michael Powell, but which, years later, is hailed as a masterpiece. The film hasn't changed, so why have the opinions of film viewers and critics changed so significantly over time?

The notoriety of *Peeping Tom* has coloured the way that we now interpret the facts of its original release and subsequent rehabilitation – a film that ruins its director then disappears only to be discovered and rereleased by a famous American director. It's a great story, but is it a true representation of *Peeping Tom*'s history?

When *Peeping Tom* was released in May 1960 the critical response was so unequivocally awful that the worst of the reviews have been written about and repeated in film histories and documentaries ever since. Although it had a dark and violent story, Michael Powell seems to have been shocked and surprised by the almost universally negative response to his film.

In his autobiography *Million Dollar Movie*, Powell wrote:

> We came, all innocently, to the opening at the Plaza Cinema, just around the corner from Piccadilly. It was owned by Paramount, and is a florid and friendly house. It was not an official premiere, but a lot of people in the business were there. Carl and I wore black tie, and I think I even sported a buttonhole. When the show was over we waited in the lobby with our friends.

> But we had no friends. They passed us with averted gaze. It was obvious they just wanted to get off the hook, go home and forget about it – and us. (Powell, 1986: 402)

This is how Carl Böehm (who played the film's main character, the killer Mark Lewis) described the same event, in an interview for the 1997 documentary *A Very British Psycho*:

> The first time when I remember I saw it, was when I came to London for the official opening. What then happened I can never forget in my life. There were some very famous people invited as honorable guests, and Mickey Powell and myself, we stood outside in the foyer, and when the film finished there was an absolute deadly

silence and we stood there and the doors opened and first at the doors were the honorable guests […] And then they came down, and they walked towards us, and suddenly they turned to the left, and they went outside even without looking at us— without shaking hands, oh well forget it, but they weren't even looking at us […] We were speechless, we looked at each other, we waited till somebody at least would comment…but nothing.

Following this critical mauling (which we will look at in detail) the film did get a very limited release in Britain but was essentially abandoned and failed to receive proper distribution. In the US the film was given a limited release, heavily edited, on the 'grindhouse' cinema circuit, and later, on TV, in an even more debased cut. The effect this reaction to *Peeping Tom* had was to limit the funding possibilities for any new projects Powell wanted to make in the UK, and it would eventually ruin his hitherto near spotless reputation as a director, making him an outcast in the British film industry – which, at the start of the 1960s, was about to undergo significant change.

BRITAIN IN 1960

In order to understand both the background to Powell making the film, and the reception it got, we need to look at the context in which it was made and released. *Peeping Tom* was filmed in 1959 and released (in the UK) in 1960. Britain in 1960 was not yet the swinging '1960s Britain' as subsequent generations have come to understand it. It was 1950s Britain just gradually starting to change. Both economically and culturally, Britain was in the shadow of the USA following the crippling damage (economic and structural) caused by the Second World War, echoes of which were still being felt socially, through conscription, which ended that year.

Yet the country *was* starting to change, in fundamental ways. In February 1960 Prime Minister Harold Macmillan made his 'Winds of Change' speech: 'The wind of change is blowing through this continent. Whether we like it or not, this growth of national consciousness is a political fact.' In 1960 60,000 people attended a demonstration in London against nuclear weapons. The general public, but particularly young people, were beginning to face up to the government and become politically engaged. Young people were instigating change rather than following their elders. There was a real feeling that the British Empire was coming to an end, which lead to a crisis of national identity – one consequence of which would be the emergence of the 'swinging sixties', resulting in a much more permissive screen culture, unfortunately several years too late for *Peeping Tom* to gain wider acceptance.

In *Studying the British Cinema: the 1960s*, Danny Powell writes:

> In film-making which shows awareness of audience motivations and the role of the cinema, the *Peeping Tom* of the title, Mark forces his victims to do exactly that, reflecting back fears both in the micro level of the story, with the use of his camera, blade and mirror but also on a macro level, reflecting the terrors of a society plummeting headlong into an age of uncertainties. It is this fear of a society without clear class divisions, of 'us' and 'them', that marks the character of this new age. (Powell, 2009: 25)

In terms of class it is difficult to place *Peeping Tom*. Many 'New Wave' British films, both before and after this, would be focussed on class – giving the working-class a newly prominent role and also highlighting the class divisions between the North and the South of Britain. But *Peeping Tom* looks at class in a very oblique way.

Mark and Helen are definitely middle-class – but they show how the concept of 'middle-class' in 1959/1960 is stretching beyond the established classification. Mark and Helen are upper- middle-class fallen on hard times. Mark is the son of an academic, but he has had to sub-divide and sub-let his family home. He himself is doing a job that he learned through an apprenticeship (in the studio) rather than at university.

From a class point of view Mark disrupts the accepted norm because in the sex trade the convention is that the working classes produce while the middle and upper classes consume. We can hear the difference in accents between the prostitutes and sex workers and their clients or employers. Mark is on the wrong side of the line, because he is involved in the production side of the porn trade, creating images and not consuming them.

Helen too is stretching the definition of middle-class. She works for a living and shares a flat with her single, alcoholic mother. There are questions about her background that are never addressed.

The world of *Peeping Tom* certainly reflects the blurring of the traditional class divisions of the period, and even though this was neither a central theme in the film, nor the real focus of the negative reviews the film received, it highlights one way in which Powell exposes fractures which were occurring in contemporary society at the time the film was made.

Another key change in 1960s Britain would be the growing importance of youth culture. Mark and Helen represent a shift in this direction but they are still a far cry from the scarily confident youth icons that dominated films of the later 1960s. Mark and Helen have failed to break free from their parents and the society which the older generation has created.

Films released even a few years later (*The Knack* in 1965, *Blow-Up*, 1966, *If*, 1968…) would have seemed impossibly avant-garde and unpalatable to a 1960 audience, and may well have been rejected in the same fashion *Peeping Tom* was. In the later '60s and into the '70s it is youth culture that would redefine Britain, both at home and internationally, and not the middle-aged critics who savaged *Peeping Tom*. The opinion and influence of these critics would become less valued and less significant as the decade wore on, and it's notable that even at the time, while the film critics mainly hated *Peeping Tom* the trade papers gave a far more measured response (see below).

The established rules of sexual morality and gender were also being transformed at this time. In 1960 Penguin Chapter Books was found not guilty of obscenity at the Old Bailey for publishing *Lady Chatterley's Lover*, 200,000 copies of which were sold in one day following its publication.[1] The contraceptive pill was released for use in the US in 1960 (and became available in Britain by 1961, but only to married women).

Through the 1950s British films had lionised the uniformed ultra-masculine heroes of the Second World War. *Peeping Tom* was made at a time when attitudes towards male gender identity and sexual identity were changing and becoming less rigid. Neither Mark in *Peeping Tom* nor Norman in *Psycho* (1960) could be defined as 'gay', but they do certainly differ from conventional male stereotypes of the time. In Britain, the Wolfenden report had, in 1957, kick-started a process that would in 1967 lead to new legislation that decriminalised homosexuality.

Given all this, had *Peeping Tom* been released later in the 1960s, there is a case to be made that it would have been regarded as less controversial. But in May 1960, the British newspaper and magazine film critics simply did not know what to make of it.

THE REVIEWS

Even though reviews in the trade press and abroad would not be nearly so damning, the critical response from many British newspaper critics was so bad that *Peeping Tom* would be denied a proper release. Being pulled from general distribution meant that only a small number of cinemagoers outside of London were ever given the opportunity to see the film at the cinema in 1960. But many of the most vitriolic reviews from the British critics tell us nothing really about *why* the film was reviled in such a way.

Derek Hill wrote in the *Tribune*: 'The only really satisfactory way to dispose of *Peeping Tom* would be to shovel it up and flush it swiftly down the nearest sewer. Even then the stench would remain.'

William Whitebait wrote in *The New Statesman*: '*Peeping Tom* stinks more than anything else in British films since *The Stranglers of Bombay* .... What worries me is that anyone could entertain this muck and give it commercial shape' (April 9, 1960).

It is ironic that even Terence Fisher, the most well-known of the Hammer horror directors, is reported to have said, '*Peeping Tom*? Horrible! From a moral point of view, of course. It is an extremely well-made film, but a bit hard to support… I would say that this sort of film is potentially dangerous' (in Green, 1996).

There are more reviews similar to these, uniformly negative and dismissive, and it is these notices that many film historians have chosen to reprint and discuss when writing about *Peeping Tom*. However, before we look more closely at why the British film critics reacted the way they did, we must acknowledge that the contemporary response to *Peeping Tom* was more nuanced than subsequent writers have allowed.

For example, this contemporary review, printed in *Picture Show*, does a great job of highlighting the contradictions that made *Peeping Tom* such a hard film for a contemporary viewer to comprehend. It acknowledges both the horror of the plot, but also the expert direction and well-judged dramatic performances:

> The **nastiest** horror film to be produced for a long time is this **controversial** and **very shocking** story of an unbalanced young man and the victims who fall prey to his camera and knife. **Beautifully produced and directed** by Michael Powell the film opens with the murder of a prostitute and gets **progressively more scary and sick-making** as the story continues. Carl **Böehm sensitively portrays** the title role of a young photographer who owes his **nauseating obsession** to photograph **terror** to his brilliant scientist father who had used his small son as a guinea pig in psychological experiments. Anna Massey gives the young man friendship and luckily escapes the fate of Moira Shearer, who appears much too briefly, along with Pamela Green and Brenda Bruce. **A gruesome climax which really scared me** (I was very hesitant about turning my light off that night) is **superbly suspenseful** but rounds up a **rather unhealthy** film which I **strongly do not recommend** to anyone in the least bit affected by what they see on screen. (*Picture Show*, 28 May 1960; author's highlights)

Compared to the newspaper film critic write-ups, the 1960 British trade publications, and the international film press also had a more balanced and positive view of the film. Take these excerpts from British trade reviews:

> That expert movie-maker Michael Powell has invested it with a maximum of technical excellence and all the quality of which he is capable. (*The Daily Cinema*, 1 April 1960)

> Psychopathic thriller, photographed in Eastmancolor, illustrating case history of brilliant young photographer turned pornographer and sadistic killer. Tale thoughtful as well as sensational, Carl Böehm outstanding, romance and humour appropriate, and climax both tragic and showman like. … It should fascinate and grip the majority. And what a title! First-rate British 'shocker'. (*Kinematograph Weekly*, 7 April 1960)

As an example of a foreign contemporary view, the 1959 review of the film in American magazine *Variety* has none of the outraged disgust common to the British reviews:

> Powell has directed with imagination but he might well have tightened up the story line. The standout feature of *Peeping Tom* is some fascinating photography by Otto Heller, particularly in the film studio sequences. His use of color and shadow is most effective. (*Variety*, 31 December 1959)

A Dutch review written by D. Ouwendijk for *De Linie* (January 1961) commented that 'The film succeeds in presenting the main issue of pain through mental illness. And doing that *Peeping Tom* distances itself a long way from the average exciting thriller.'

The French film press, which in the late 1950s and early '60s would become so important in shaping our understanding of film (via the emergence of film theory and the auteur theory) gave a more equivocal view of *Peeping Tom*. Film writer and director Bertrand Tavernier later became a friend of Michael Powell and would become instrumental in championing his work in France, while, in his review for the French magazine *Positif*, Jean-Paul Torok wrote,

Certain moments achieve a quite extraordinary sort of black poetry: the excerpts from the father's experimental films are bathed in the sheer light of terror, and the presence of the lizard in the child's bed is enough to tell us all that needs to be told about onanism and the castration complex. Thanks to skilful lighting effects, the murder in the studio is disturbingly effective. Lewis' final suicide, spectacular enough in itself, is accompanied by impressive funeral rites: police sirens, screaming children recorded on tape, flashbulbs exploding, cries of horror and assorted noises. As for the humour, it is cleverly used to enhance the moments of inaction. (Torok, *Positif* 36, 1960)

Perhaps foreign critics were able to be more apparently objective because the film was set in Britain (not 'home'), and many of the finer points Powell makes in the film (for example, his exposé of the sex trade and snipes at the hypocrisy of the British middle-classes) were specifically aimed at a British audience. But let us take a closer look at the domestic reviews to try and glean a clearer indication of what it was exactly that the critics hated so much about the film.

THE PROBLEM WITH MICHAEL POWELL

Dilys Powell, the critic for *The Sunday Times*, was one of the most influential critics in Britain. Her opinion really mattered. In her 1960 review she wrote of *Peeping Tom* that,

It is made by a director of skill and sensibility, the same stylist's view it is which now and then makes the torturer's stuff of the new film look like the true imaginative thing, the Edgar Allan Poe horror, instead of the vulgar squalor it really is. The director whose daring and inquiring eye gave us the superb camera obscura sequence and the entry into the operating room in *A Matter of Life and Death*. Then one remembers that even in his best period Michael Powell would suddenly devote his gifts to a story about a maniac who poured glue over girls' hair. He has got beyond glue here. He has got to the trick knife lovingly embedded in the throat, to the voyeur with sound effects, to a nauseating emphasis on the preliminaries and the practice of sadism – and I mean sadism. He did not write *Peeping Tom*; but he cannot wash his hands of responsibility for this essentially vicious film. (10 April 1960)

Dilys Powell writes a very personal review which criticises Michael Powell himself rather than picking out any specific scenes in the actual film that are problematic for her. She seems to feel personally betrayed by him, because she rates him as a talented director. But she was not the only critic who reacted in this way. Isabel Quigley of the *Spectator* wrote:

Mr Michael Powell (who once made such outstanding films as *Black Narcissus* and *A Matter of Life and Death*) produced and directed *Peeping Tom* and I think he ought to be ashamed of himself. The acting is good. The photography is fine. But what is the result as I saw it on the screen? Sadism, sex and the exploitation of human degradation. (15 April 1960)

Yet another example of this approach was written by Len Mosely in the *Daily Express*:

Anyone who can think up a plot starting like this must have a peculiar sort of mind. But what can you say about a man who considers this is a suitable subject to turn into a film? You can praise him if it becomes a work of art. But condemnation should be doubly strong if the film that emerges disgusts and repels. (8 April 1960)

And Nina Hibbin in *The Daily Worker*

…was shocked to the core to find a director of his standing befouling the screen with such perverted nonsense. It wallows in the diseased urges of a homicidal pervert ... It uses phoney cinema artifice and heavy orchestral music to whip up a debased atmosphere ... From its lumbering, mildly salacious beginning to its appallingly masochistic and depraved climax, it is wholly evil. (9 April 1960)

The criticism aimed at Powell rather than the film is something that typifies the British reviews of *Peeping Tom*. Powell, with his creative partner Emeric Pressburger (together known as 'The Archers'), had become a loved and respected creator of some of the most highly rated and popular British films of the preceding two decades. There were expectations of what a Powell film should be like, and *Peeping Tom* did not meet those expectations.

In most of the reviews Michael Powell himself was singled out as the sole author of the work, despite the fact Leo Marks was the originator of the story and wrote the screenplay. Although the 'auteur theory' had yet to find widespread acceptance, the influence of, especially French, writers on film that identified the director as the key creative influence behind a film was gaining currency. While Powell did not necessarily identify himself as an auteur, and always talked in great detail about the importance of various collaborators in the creation of his films, there is undeniably an intense interest in the fantastical throughout his films, and a critique of establishment hypocrisy.

Powell himself recognised the personal angle of the reviews, commenting in his memoirs:

> From the critics' point of view it must have been a nightmare. No wonder that when they got me alone and out on a limb with *Peeping Tom*, they gleefully sawed off the limb and jumped up and down on the corpse. So, it was Powell all the time, eh? We suspected Emeric Pressburger with his Continental background, but now we know it was Powell, the sadist, who poured glue on girls' hair, or splashed buckets of blood all over Moira Shearer lying on the railroad tracks when she should have been allowed to die neatly and tidily, like a British ballerina. Let's go get him! (1986: 143)

To what extent is *Peeping Tom* Michael Powell's film? Are Powell and Leo Marks equally responsible for it? Would Marks' screenplay have resulted in a less controversial film if it had been filmed by someone else or Powell had used a pseudonym on the credits? Maybe Pressburger had tempered the darker elements of Powell's imagination, whereas Leo Marks had encouraged them? These are questions we cannot definitively answer but contemporary critics seem in the main to have ignored Marks' role in its creation.

POWELL VERSUS THE CRITICS

Another strand of criticism found across several contemporary *Peeping Tom* reviews is that the critics recognised the fact that to some extent Powell was implicating the viewer, and by extension the professional critic, of sharing Mark's perversion.

A critic is someone who is paid to watch – a professional voyeur. Powell's film makes the viewer/critic complicit in the crime by using subjective point-of-view shots from the very start. The fact that the viewer *becomes* the killer and is unable to pull away is, perhaps, a key to why critics were so disgusted and repelled by the film.

Leo Marks may have written the murder scenes but it was Powell who chose how to shoot them, and as I argue elsewhere in this book, the camerawork is absolutely key in understanding why the first viewers (critics and otherwise) reacted with such a strong sense of revulsion.

Danny Powell notes that 'The implication in *Peeping Tom* that cinema is an unhealthy past time connected with the perception of a mass audience, seeking thrills without guilt, is at the centre of the text and the film's self-awareness constantly reminds the audience of their part in the "entertainment". If the entertainments of the mass age are salacious, it is only a reflection of those who crave it' (2009: 29).

Critics and ordinary viewers (the few who saw it) reacted against *Peeping Tom* because of the way the film made them feel about themselves, and maybe also the society they lived in. The person watching the film shared the perverted and curious gaze of the killer, rather than the innocent, blameless and passive position of the victim. Powell was breaking some very subtle but well-established cinematic rules here, and probably the biggest is that the viewer exists entirely outside the world of the film and cannot be implicated in anything that happens within it.

Michael Powell makes the viewer question their own motivation, but he takes the explicit attack on critics themselves a bit further. An example of this is a scene where we see the managing director of the studio where Mark works, a secondary story in the film, talking on the phone. His name is Don Jarvis (similar to that of the real-life Rank Organisation MD, John Davis) and the caller mentions 'Kenny and Alec', a cheeky reference to two of Rank's biggest stars of the '50s, Kenneth More and Alec Guinness.

Throughout, the scenes set in the studio portray it as being a place where profits are the only important thing and the films being made are of low quality.

Powell uses these scenes partly to ease tension in between murders, but in doing so he openly ridicules the Rank Organisation, which dominated the British film establishment of the 1950s. The British film industry at that time was predominantly turning out cheap popular films of little artistic ambition. Powell criticises a system which was withholding the funding and artistic freedom he once enjoyed to make films the way he wants to make them. According to Powell, in 1947, J Arthur Rank told 'The Archers' in a meeting, 'Next year we'll be alright, but now we've got to go to the banks and borrow the money for production and pay them interest. You boys are spending a lot of money on this new picture of yours, and we expect you to make sacrifices' (Powell, 1986: 647). However, it was this same system that the established newspaper film critics were also a key part of, and arguably complicit in, so his pointed attack on the establishment may well have rankled with the critics who helped prop that system up.

THE IMPACT OF THE CRITICAL RESPONSE

The impact of the negative critical response in 1960 was immediate and devastating, for the fortunes of the film itself and also its director. Michael Powell in an interview conducted by Richard Jameson in 1989 commented:

> Then they showed it to the critics and booked to go and needed to go into a big cinema, and such a scream went up that hasn't happened since Sodom and Gomorrah. They ruined it, they made me take it off the cinema, take it off the circuit, the distribution was canceled, and the producer sold the rights, or television rights, to America. Somebody almost immediately went bankrupt, and the film disappeared for nearly 20 years. (In Lazar, 2003: 167)

In this excerpt from an interview Michael Powell gave to Rolande Lacourbe and Danièle Grivel in 1977, it is possible to see the extent to which Powell was shocked and hurt by the reaction to *Peeping Tom*, and its subsequent impact on his career:

> The reception of the film? A disaster for me! It was the end of me with a generation of distributors and cinema owners. They said, 'If Powell can't touch a film of horror

and violence without making an artistic masterpiece, without even talking about "scopophilia," without creating a human tragedy, without being full of compassion for the insane and the unhinged, there's nothing more to be done with him!'

I was very surprised. I was–I am–innocent and I thought my intentions were clear enough. When the critics reviled me, I didn't answer. All you have to do is read them: it was a frenzied attack. [...] The film truly ruined me: after it, it was impossible to get funds for other projects. The fact that *Peeping Tom* is accepted today as 'Doctor Powell's Testament' changes nothing. (In Lazar, 2003: 64)

It is undeniably true that *Peeping Tom* had a devastating impact on Powell's career in Britain. After 1960 he was unable to find funding at home for his own projects. He did make some films, but he had lost the reputation that had enabled him to make what he chose. It is generally argued that *Peeping Tom* was the reason this happened, but it is perhaps naïve to think that a single film was the only cause, because by 1960 Powell's career was already on a downward curve. His celebrated partnership with Emeric Pressburger as The Archers, was, if not formally ended, then certainly on a hiatus.

The Archers had formed in 1943 during what turned out to be a short-lived bubble of opportunity for film-makers in Britain. J Arthur Rank included them amongst his 'Independent Producers' – a group of talented film directors and producers to whom he gave creative carte blanche and the necessary funds to make what they liked. He felt confident he could do that because at that time the British government had legislated to reduce the impact of American films dominating the market and cinema attendance was very high. But this situation was artificially created and unfortunately didn't last.

Rank had given The Archers the freedom to make films that were expensive and creatively experimental, not predictable and genre-driven. But when Rank's finances began to falter, control of film production was largely given over to John Davis, an accountant who had little interest in contributing to film as an art. In his essay, 'Peeping Tom: The Myths', Steve Crook writes, 'by the 1960s, [...] Rank had almost been bankrupted by some expensive films like Gabby Pascal's *Caesar and Cleopatra* (1948) and then by over-extending in the American market. J. Arthur Rank had been forced to step aside and the company was run by the accountant John Davis who had had previous run-ins with Powell.'[2]

Davis favoured cheap sequels and genre films that had a reliable box office – no chances could be taken, especially with the hugely ambitious ideas people like Michael Powell had. So by 1960 Michael Powell's career was already in trouble because he was not making the kinds of films that film financiers in Britain wanted to take a risk by paying for (Bloom Walden, 2013: 47-50).

In *Peeping Tom*, Powell uses the scenes set at the film studio to openly criticise and ridicule the mainstream British film industry that would no longer give him what he wanted. In her notes for the Criterion 1994 laserdisc release of *Peeping Tom*, Laura Mulvey comments that, '*Peeping Tom*'s portrait of Pinewood Studios is a farcical, bitter, almost vengeful picture of an industry's total complacency in the face of creative and economic decline. Powell, knowing that The Archers represented the best of British cinema, deeply resented their marginalization.'

It is disingenuous to argue, as some writers have, that *Peeping Tom* single-handedly ended Powell's career, but it did bring his fading career to a more dramatic stop than might have occurred otherwise. Powell did continue to work after 1960. After *Peeping Tom*, he went on to make his last UK feature film, *The Queen's Guards* in 1961, then had some success making two films in Australia, *They're a Weird Mob* (1966) and *Age of Consent* (1969). He also made smaller projects, working with Emeric Pressburger once again on the 1972 children's film *The Boy Who Turned Yellow* (1972).

And it is worth noting that although *Peeping Tom* is widely believed to have had a devastating effect on Powell's career, it does not seem to have had the same effect on the actors who brought it to life. Notably, Carl Böehm worked for Disney and MGM within the same period, so he was not tarred or tarnished by playing Mark Lewis (perhaps because of his depiction of Mark as an innocent of sorts). And Anna Massey's role as Helen, though less controversial did not harm her career (indeed, it is hard to believe Hitchcock's casting of her in the London-set *Frenzy* (1972) is accidental; it is almost a spiritual reprise of her *Peeping Tom* character, albeit older if not wiser).

In making *Peeping Tom*, Powell seems to have been knowingly trying to make something quite different from anything he had done before – he knew he was defying expectations in doing so and he was willing to take that risk. The noted film editor Thelma Schoonmaker (later Powell's wife) has said that 'Michael completely reinvented his filmmaking style in *Peeping Tom* – an incredibly daring and courageous decision'. But she also points out:'Michael felt that if you were at the cutting edge of your art you had to understand that it was a dangerous place to be, and that history was filled with brilliant artists whose careers had been destroyed by the fact that they "went too far"' (unpublished correspondence with author).

We've started our review of the history *Peeping Tom* with the aftermath of its release. Now it is time to go back to the start.

FOOTNOTES

1. https://www.bl.uk/learning/timeline/item105907.html
2. Essay at Powell-Pressburger.org

CHAPTER 2: MAKING *PEEPING TOM*

'I have never known a more electric atmosphere than on the set of *Peeping Tom*.' – Anna Massey

Peeping Tom is, of course, a film by Michael Powell and resolutely *not* one made in partnership with Emeric Pressburger under the banner of The Archers. However, it was made only two years after the last of the Archers productions. In 1942 Pressburger had laid out The Archers 'manifesto' in a letter to the actress Wendy Hiller. Reading it gives us important insight into the approach Powell later took when he was making *Peeping Tom*.

One, we owe allegiance to nobody except the financial interests which provide our money; and, to them, the sole responsibility of ensuring them a profit, not a loss.

Two, every single foot in our films is our own responsibility and nobody else's. We refuse to be guided or coerced by any influence but our own judgement.

Three, when we start work on a new idea we must be a year ahead, not only of our competitors, but also of the times. A real film, from idea to universal release, takes a year. Or more.

Four, no artist believes in escapism. And we secretly believe that no audience does. We have proved, at any rate, that they will pay to see the truth, for other reasons than her nakedness.

Five, at any time, and particularly at the present, the self-respect of all collaborators, from star to prop-man, is sustained, or diminished, by the theme and purpose of the film they are working on. They will fight or intrigue to work on a subject they feel is urgent or contemporary, and fight equally hard to avoid working on a trivial or pointless subject. And we agree with them and want the best workmen with us; and get them.

These are the main things we believe in. They have brought us an unbroken record of success and a unique position. Without the one, of course, we should not enjoy the other very long. We are under no illusions. We know we are surrounded by hungry sharks. But you have no idea what fun it is surf-bathing, if you have only paddled, with a nurse holding on to the back of your rompers.

We hope you will come on in, the water's fine.

(In MacDonald, 1994: 189-190)

The first point highlights the fact (as do several other remarks made by Powell in interviews and his autobiographies) that even though in his career with Pressburger he was not known for making mainstream films per se, he certainly never set out to make one that did not have the potential to be financially successful.

Point two shows that whether Powell considered himself to be an auteur or not, the way he had always approached a project was with the understanding that overall the whole film was his own responsibility. Powell was always keen to collaborate with others in the development of a film, but when it came to shooting it, he had (and needed to have) complete confidence to take charge. As Thelma Schoonmaker comments, 'once he had a film ready to shoot, he probably felt he had to have a firm hand on how the film is made – any good director feels that way' (from unpublished correspondence with the author).

Point three shows the artistic ambition (of The Archers and Powell himself) to be ahead of the pack – something that in hindsight has been said again and again by critics in relation to *Peeping Tom*. In fact, points three to five give us an idea of why Powell chose to make *Peeping Tom* at all. It fulfils Powell and Pressburger's commitment to new ideas that are ahead of the times, to represent truth rather than escapism and is certainly a film on a subject that could be considered 'urgent' and contemporary rather than trivial or pointless.

Point five also shows how Powell was dedicated to making sure that his film represented its subject as well as possible. Whatever film he was working on, Powell was always entirely dedicated to bringing it to the screen as perfectly as possible and he felt that a film with a worthy enough subject would lead its crew to work on it with the same devotion.

The final comments, about swimming in shark-infested waters make one final point. Nearly two decades later, Powell was well aware that *Peeping Tom* was a risky film to make. But he wanted to take risks with his film-making, 'paddling' held no attraction to him, so he went ahead and made it anyway.

It can be very hard to find first-hand accounts of what it was like 'behind the scenes' on the making of a film decades after it was completed. In the case of *Peeping Tom* we have to piece together information from a number of autobiographies and a few contemporary photographs. We can collate these accounts and come to some conclusions but it is always worth remembering the unavoidable bias of personal accounts, especially when they are written in memoirs published years after the events they recall.

BRINGING THE SCREENPLAY TO THE SCREEN

In 1959 Powell would have been trying to establish his solo career as quite separate from the celebrated brand name he had jointly set up with Emeric Pressburger. The Archers were Powell and Pressburger, so in effect Powell was starting from scratch with his solo ventures. *Peeping Tom* marked a new direction, and having had such success with his creative partner Powell was looking for a new project and potentially a new collaborator.

Unlike Powell's old working partner Emeric Pressburger, Leo Marks was not someone with a track record working in the film industry. This rather enigmatic man was the son of a book dealer (the owner of the famous 84 Charing Cross Road). Marks had spent the war working with the Special Operations Executive. There, as head of code development and code security, he started to write poems. These were used as unique codes given to individual operatives. His most famous poem, written for Violette Szabo later became known in the film *Carve Her Name with Pride* (1958).

Powell's working relationship with Marks seems to some extent to have mimicked his relationship with Pressburger. Thelma Schoonmaker says that 'I am not really sure why Michael chose *Peeping Tom* after his partnership with Emeric broke up. He would have needed a writer and maybe he felt that Leo Marks had interesting ideas and was someone with whom he could co-write the script. I think Michael participated in the writing of the films of The Archers much more than people realise. He maybe felt that he and Leo could work well in tandem on the project, and it seems that they did' (unpublished correspondence with the author).

Michael Powell and Leo Marks initially came together with the intention of working on ideas for a film about Freud. But they abandoned that project having heard of another Freud film in the pipeline to be directed by John Huston. Instead they went back to the drawing board, with an idea Marks came up with and Powell immediately leaped on with enthusiasm.

In his autobiography, Powell remembers that '[Marks] sat down, leant towards me, fixed me with a penetrating gaze, and said, "Mr Powell, how would you like to make a film about a young man with a camera who kills the women that he photographs?" I said, "That's me. I'd like it very much"' (1986: 393).

It's significant that Leo Marks wrote *Peeping Tom* already knowing who was going to direct it, and with some direct input from Powell as it was being written. He wrote it *for* Powell and that fact leads him to highlight what we might recognise as the meta aspects of the story – a film about filming, a director making a film about directing. However, Marks clearly wrote aspects of himself into the film too, most obviously naming the central character Mark Lewis after himself. It seems that both men felt more than usually attached to the story they created. Authorship is of central importance to the auteur theory but while some consider Powell to have been an auteur, Leo Marks had a huge role in the creation of *Peeping Tom*.

Marks and Powell seem to have been a good match for each other. According to interviewer Luke Jennings, during the Second World War Marks was turned down as a code-breaker for Bletchley Park on the grounds of his 'facetiousness and unorthodoxy', two characteristics which could all too easily also be applied to Michael Powell. In his autobiography, Powell remarks that 'Leo was an ideal creative partner. He knew nothing about films or the theatre, but a very great deal about men and women. He was malicious, inventive and unshockable' (1986: 395).

This book is not the place for a detailed comparison of the finished film and the original screenplay. But there are many subtle differences between the two, and it is in finding these differences that you pinpoint why Powell is considered to be an auteur. Every little change he makes from what Marks wrote adds Powell's own style to the film, and gives it a level of technical and artistic shine not present on the pages of Leo Marks' original script.

Marks wrote a story about a filmmaker, but he himself was not a filmmaker. Powell's interpretation of the screenplay added an extra level of depth and believability to the character of Mark. The way he approached making the film was very much influenced by his own feelings towards the art of film-making and his personal experience of trying to navigate the various hurdles of the British film industry. (This is no doubt also why the film has become a favourite among film directors.)

Once Powell and Marks finished working on the script, Powell set about making the film, delighting himself with the technicalities of film-making. Powell's second wife, film editor Thelma Schoonmaker has described the satisfaction Powell took in working out how to film the scene which features pencils that fall out of Mark's pocket as he stands on the gantry in the film studio. It is not a hugely important shot, yet Powell experimented with film speeds and giant prop pencils to make sure he captured the action just as he wanted it. This shines a light on the aspects of filming he really enjoyed – getting technical details right so that every shot was as good as it could be. Powell boasted that the famed producer Alexander Korda had told him 'Mickey is the greatest technician in the movies!' (Powell, M., 1986: 497).

What Powell made was a technically brilliant film that was faithful to the ideas of the screenplay. If it didn't elicit the response from viewers that he was hoping for, this is because he had high expectations of his audience, expecting them to understand and appreciate the story he was telling, connecting to the story on an intellectual and emotional level. In fact Powell packed in many levels of detail that any ordinary viewer would be very unlikely to register, including casting a blind actor (Esmond Knight) to play the 'film within a film' studio film director.

Peeping Tom was financed and distributed (or as it turned out, *not* distributed) by Anglo-Amalgamated. The company was known through the '50s for low-budget 'B'-type movies. Financing *Peeping Tom* was part of a move they were making in the early '60s to try and work with well-known film talent and move away from their low-quality reputation. They wanted to work with Powell because of his impressive CV, but ultimately, they would not be supportive when the critics wrote the film off as a shocking horror film instead of the piece of art by a well-known director they had envisaged.

CASTING

Casting will always have a huge effect on the tone of a film, and Powell chose the cast of *Peeping Tom* film carefully, but many would say unconventionally. In a 1989 interview with Richard Jameson, Michael Powell was asked about the casting of the film and replied flippantly, 'You don't want to hear about casting, that was in the normal way' (in Lazar, 2003: 167). But in saying that, Powell underplays how important casting was to him (it was something he had a great talent for) and also how the casting of this film in particular was in some aspects quite out of the ordinary.

Of his lead, Carl Böehm, Powell said, 'I met him by chance. He was exactly the right mixture of innocence and completely loony. Very touching. Very moving. And it was really for me a very compassionate and interesting film about a man' (ibid.). The casting of Böehm as Mark was both inspired and unconventional – although Böehm was a well-regarded actor in non-English language films, an established British star might have leant the film more commercial clout. Several well-known British actors are reported to have turned the role down before Böehm was cast.

The original screenplay does not say Mark is anything other than English. Carl Böehm's soft but noticeable accent is never explained in the film, but gives him a foreign rather than boy-next-door quality – a slight other-ness that changes the way the audience relates to him. The Germanic tones of his accent would, in post-war England, have given him a slightly sinister edge and aurally link him to Fritz Lang's lead in *M* (1931), Peter Lorre.

Helen, arguably the other most important role in the film, is, in the screenplay, a rather ordinary example of a pretty young female lead. Helen was only Anna Massey's second film role, and her first lead. Like Mark's part, the role in the original screenplay is less complex than it became when Powell cast it. Helen could have been a straightforward girl-next-door. In the script she is first described as, 'CLOSE SHOT of dear HELEN. A sensitive, intelligent, and extremely attractive girl.' But Anna Massey brings the role greater depth, coming across like a curious bird, quick witted and unconventional (qualities which later characterised the heroines of 1980s slashers).

Anna Massey said in her memoirs that 'It was the most wonderful part, full of emotion, warmth and innocence' (2006: 76). She went on to say, of her experience working on the film: 'The filming of *Peeping Tom* was an absorbing time for me. My father's old friend Michael Powell was an extraordinary man. He came to the set each day immaculately dressed, a distinguished ferret in a tweed suit and a bow tie. He thrived on tension. I have never known a more electric atmosphere than on the set of *Peeping Tom*' (ibid.).

Another very significant piece of unusual casting was Moira Shearer as the aspiring starlet Vivian. In the film script Vivian is an important victim – we see more of her character than we do of some other victims – but it is still a relatively small role. She is written as a straightforward and perhaps slightly desperate bit-part actress who is trying to work her way up into larger roles and stardom. Powell's choice of Moira Shearer for the role is surprising.

Fig 1 Moira Shearer was the biggest star of the film, but she plays the part of a small-time actress who becomes just another of Mark's victims. The fact she was such a well-loved star made her murder in the film more shocking for a contemporary audience to watch. © StudioCanal.

At the time it was made, Moira Shearer was by far the biggest star in the cast. So again, there is an ironic humour in her playing a woman who desperately wants to be a star. Shearer was maybe older than the part was written. There is something very unsettling both about the onscreen killing of a well-loved British star, and also the unquestioning obedience with which her character acquiesces with Mark's requests when he is filming her – because she is older than him, and as audience members identify, in reality she is better known and more experienced than him.

Shearer also links *Peeping Tom* with two of Powell's most famous and successful films of the past, *The Red Shoes* (1948) and *Tales of Hoffman* (1951). It underlines the fact that Powell was proud of *Peeping Tom* – by casting Shearer he unapologetically includes the film in his canon of past work.

When it came to the publicity for the film, a whole series of publicity images exist which feature Powell with his son Columba, Carl Böehm and Shearer. Massey is not included in this series of photographs and it points to the fact that Shearer was a bigger draw than Anna Massey, who in the context of this film had a far more important role. It is not clear whether this particular publicity shoot might have been influenced by the financial backers and distributors, keen to try and protect their investment by making the most of the film's best-known star.

Again, undermining his own assertion that casting was irrelevant, Powell's choice of actors for even the smaller roles is very significant. The older man who comes to the shop to buy a (respectable broadsheet) newspaper but then asks for 'views' is played by Miles Malleson. He was a well-loved character actor who would have been familiar to any British audience. Powell casts Malleson because he knows that British viewers will associate him with characters he has played in previous movies. The casting underlines the point Powell is making in this scene. He is using the scene to expose the hypocrisy of so called 'respectable' society. He shows a middle-class man (as evidenced by how he is dressed, and the fact he is called 'Sir' by the shopkeeper) buying porn photographs, which he then covers with two broadsheet newspapers, *The Times* and *The Telegraph*. This scene, and the way it was cast and written is another example of Powell using cultural references that a British audience might take exception to but a foreign viewer would be very likely to miss entirely.

Fig 2 This somewhat misleading publicity suggests Moira Shearer has a much bigger role than she actually had, and Columba looks disarmingly innocent. The image implies 'Great director at work with the star of his previous hits'. © StudioCanal.

META-CASTING – POWELL AS MARK'S FATHER, AND COLUMBA POWELL AS YOUNG MARK

In *Peeping Tom*, we see films within the film, black-and-white home movies taken by Mark's father to document the research he is doing on his son. Powell chose to cast himself as Mark's father, and his own son Columba as the young Mark. He also used his first wife Frankie in shots of Mark's dead mother, and filmed these scenes mainly in or near the family home.

From a purely practical point of view one can see how directing your own son might be easier than working with a child actor. Powell himself said of casting Columba, 'I felt it gave the whole thing a greater truth than if we had a routine child actor. My son understood what we were doing – I explained it all to him – and enjoyed doing it' (quoted in 'Mr. Michael Powell on Making Horror Films', *The Thunderer*, 5 July 1960).

Some critics seem to have interpreted this casting as another example of Powell's twisted imagination. They took exception to it, thinking that it was wrong for him to

Fig 3 Powell and his son Columba on set. In memoirs and interviews both Columba and Michael Powell recall enjoying filming Peeping Tom *together.* © StudioCanal.

expose his own son to such dark subject matter. They thought that by casting himself as Dr Lewis he must in some way condone the Doctor's sadistic research, submitting his own real-life son to similar horrors to those committed in the film's narrative.

The British Board of Film Classification, in an article written for their website, states: 'The general reaction [to the film] was a mixture of repulsion and disgust – not least over the casting choice of Powell's own son, Columba, as Mark as a child, with Powell himself playing the dictatorial father of the hapless child who in adulthood becomes a serial killer. Powell had chosen to use his son in the film because he thought he would get a more realistic performance from the boy than if he had used a child actor. But there was a strong reaction to the scenes which present Mark's father conducting experiments on the child as part of his study of the psychology of terror.'[3] But although the film critics (who knew Powell well) reacted in that way it could be argued that it's likely an ordinary viewer would not have been aware of this curious meta-casting.

Michael Powell identified with *Peeping Tom* because it was a film about film-making. In a programme he made in 1985 for *The South Bank Show*, he introduces himself (with the *Peeping Tom* soundtrack playing in the background) saying: 'Peeping Tom speaking, I live

Fig 4 Here we see (in intentionally out of focus 'home movie' footage), Powell as Mark's father, with Columba Powell as young Mark. © StudioCanal.

the cinema, I chose the cinema or the cinema chose me when I was very young…' This also clarifies another way in which Powell failed to understand the difference between the audience view and his own view of the film. To Powell, Mark was a film-maker first, murderer second. As a film-maker making a film about another film-maker (albeit a psychopathic one), Powell saw Mark largely as a sympathetic character. He wanted to challenge his audience with something new and unsettling – to show that they were voyeurs. To show them a side of film-making they didn't know about. But many of the critics and ordinary viewers failed to see the subtle layers of the story Powell was presenting and they saw Mark simply as a sick killer. They could not see why Powell would paint him as such a sympathetic character, and Powell could not see why anyone would fail to see Mark sympathetically.

WORKING WITH POWELL

Judging from interviews with actors he worked with, Powell had high expectations of his crew, but the fact many of them became life-long friends shows that they generally did not resent the way he made them work on set. Another reason Powell could be a taskmaster when filming was that in a pre-digital age when every foot of film exposed added to the cost of the film, he tried to be economical and shoot as few takes as he could get away with. He expected his film crew and cast to be a team in which everyone worked as diligently as he did.

Actress Pamela Green is one of the cast members who has written in some detail about her own experience of working on the film. Many of her recollections seem to highlight Powell's uncompromising style of direction, intent always on getting the best visual effect but sometimes at the expense of his actors.

> Powell was a strange man to work with, cold, somewhat remote; a sarcastic tongue. He seemed to enjoy humiliating the actors, and certain ones would be his whipping boys and one day it was me. I had put on the flowered negligee and was standing being lit by Otto, when the storm broke. My costume was wrong. It was not transparent enough and I looked like a bale of material, (I knew that), why?... Because it had been lined with a pink lining for decency's sake [said Wardrobe]. 'Then take it out now [said Powell].' (https://pamela-green.com/essays/filming-peeping-tom/)

Green also recounted an incident where Powell needed more and more light for a shot featuring her. In the end (according to Green), against all advice, he shot the scene with arc lights that were so hot they burned her skin.

Thelma Schoonmaker confirms Powell's reputation for cruelty: 'I have heard that Michael could be pretty rough on the set. He felt filmmaking was like a religion, and when you came on his set you had damned well better be ready and do the best possible job for him, and if you didn't he could be merciless' (interview in *The Telegraph*, 25 March 2007).

Although these incidents are today unverifiable, taken together the overall impression we get is that Powell was a passionate taskmaster on set, willing to do anything to get a scene 'right'.

Anna Massey, however, is kinder in her memoirs than Pamela Green is in hers. Despite admitting that 'often on set I was genuinely scared, even though the crew were around' Massey stoically concludes that

> Like John Ford, Powell believed in setting up the shots carefully, and then, when the crew were ready, the actors would return. We would rehearse until Powell was

satisfied that he could get his shot in one take. We never did more than two. Some of the takes were eight or nine minutes long, involving extremely intricate tracking. I learnt an enormous amount about filming from Michael Powell. He was not easy to work with, but he was a true original and a task master. I think he enabled everyone to give of their best. (2006: 76)

CINEMATOGRAPHY

Whether critics choose to recognise his collaborators or not, Michael Powell always gave a great deal of credit to the technical expertise of the people he worked with. His films are often noted for remarkable cinematography and in particular his use of lighting, and in later films, colour. This of course may have been characteristic of Powell's own approach as a director but was directly possible because of his collaborations with very talented cinematographers and cameramen. On *The Red Shoes* Powell worked with legendary cinematographer Jack Cardiff, but on *Peeping Tom* he worked for the only time in his career with Otto Heller.

Fig 5 Michael Powell and the Hungarian cinematographer Otto Heller. Heller was someone who Powell had wanted to work with for some time. © StudioCanal.

Michael Powell commented that 'I'd always wanted to work with Otto Heller, I thought his work as a cameraman was wonderful' (in Lazar, 2003: 167). Anna Massey recalled in her memoirs: 'Our lighting cameraman was the great Otto Heller who had lit many of Marlene Dietrich's films. He had the most delightful and bubbly personality, not dimmed at all by his age. He adored women, and used wonderful blue filters to flatter them' (2006: 77).

Heller was born in Prague and worked in various countries before settling in Britain in 1940. In his black-and-white films he perfected a 'film noir' style characterised by high contrast and shadow, and in colour his striking work on films including *The Ladykillers* and *Richard III* (both 1955) would have suggested him as a suitable candidate to Powell for *Peeping Tom*.

It can be hard to know to what extent the camerawork in a film is the result of the camera team and/or the director, but comments made by both Pamela Green and Anna Massey imply that Powell was very directly involved in each shot, collaborating with Heller and the camera team rather than leaving them to it.

Anna Massey recalled that 'Before each take he had to have a row with someone, and it was usually the camera operator, Gerry Turpin, who was the target of his wrath. He liked to do tremendously long and complicated takes, so everyone's nerves were already on edge without the added friction provided by the director' (Massey, 2006: 76).

Looking at the original shooting script does not tell us that much more – most of the camera notes mention generic instructions 'camera pans, camera tracks' etc. in scenes which actually use the innovative hand-held point-of-view shots. So it seems that the script is not necessarily an accurate record of which camera shots were chosen, and why. There is, however, one interesting anomaly in the script. In some sections the point-of-view camera is referred to as if the camera itself is a character in the film. For example, this section, taken from the Dora murder sequence right at the start of the film:

CLOSE SHOT of Dora. She holds out her hand-smiling.

> **And suddenly. There is a gentle whirring purring sound.**

```
CAMERA HOLDS ON Dora - she is staring at something
with great curiosity.

It turns quickly to bewilderment - and the
bewilderment to fear. She steps back from CAMERA -
but CAMERA won't have it.

Dora is now staring at something in horror - she
opens her mouth to scream - a shadow falls across
her face.

The sound purrs on.⁴
```

This makes it clear that the way Powell and Marks have written the scene implies the sinister independence of the camera as an entity within the context of this story.

Looking at the lighting separate to the camera technique, Powell and Heller used Eastmancolor (which had previously been chosen for another Anglo-Amalgamated horror film, *Horrors of the Black Museum* (1959)) to create a very saturated and mostly quite unrealistic (or impressionistic) style. It is notable that *Peeping Tom* used a number of real-life locations as well as studio sets, but it can be very difficult to tell them apart because the lighting of locations such as Newman Passage, scene of the opening murder, makes it look very artificial. The result is unsettling, because the action is presented as real – but in a highly theatrical way.

Shadow is used expressively, sometimes to withhold information from the viewer – for example, hiding a character or just their face in shadow. The lighting of Helen (flat and bright) is often contrasted with the way her mother is lit with a shadowed face – maybe a visual expression of her blindness, or even the mother's suspicion towards Mark contrasted with her daughter's frank openness.

The menace achieved through the lighting (or lack of it) was, according to Anna Massey, also true in real life: 'The lighting was extremely low-key and atmospheric, and I often felt quite isolated and threatened. I am sure this was Powell's intention' (Massey, 2006: 77).

*Fig 6 Powell measures light
levels while setting up for a
shot of Pamela Green. Green
had a successful career as
a glamour model and her
experience was invaluable
to Powell when creating the
porn photo studio set.
© StudioCanal.*

MUSIC AND SOUND

In a film so much focussed on looking, the way in which sound and music are used must also be mentioned. As in so many horror films, the soundtrack for *Peeping Tom* made a significant contribution to building up the atmosphere Powell wanted, right from the opening of the film.

Brian Easdale's urgent, jazzy solo piano score was distinctive enough that some critics mention it in their reviews. For example Nina Hibben of *The Daily Worker* mis-remembered the soundtrack and wrote, 'Sparing no tricks, it uses phoney cinema artifice and heavy orchestral music to whip up a debased atmosphere' (*The Daily Worker*, April, 1960).

The diegetic sound of the film is also memorable, with some menacing sections that are silent apart from the sounds of Mark's camera or projector working. At the very start of Leo Marks' shooting script he writes, 'In the darkness WE HEAR the film's THEME MUSIC – a gentle whirring purring noise. Nothing to be alarmed about. It might be a small contented motor.' While Powell often stated that he did not consider *Peeping Tom* to be a horror film, in his use of sound he makes a direct reference to Fritz Lang's pioneering 1931 serial killer thriller, *M*. Mark stalks his first victim, walking along the street whistling – an aural device used to introduce Peter Lorre's killer in *M*.

MISE-EN-SCÈNE

Fig 7 Camera operators and Otto Heller, Powell and Carl Böehm shooting what appears to be one of Mark's hand-held shots outside on location. This was before the invention of the Steadicam, which would be used to create similar shots in later films. © StudioCanal.

When *Peeping Tom* was shown at the 1979 New York Film Festival, Elliott Stein wrote in *Film Comment*:

> Much bloodier than *Peeping Tom* were the Hammer horrors of the period – but their creators got off the critical hook far more easily. Powell's contemporary study in psychopathy did not take place over a rainbow in Transylvania. It could not be

dismissed with a cup of garlic, a cobweb, and a crucifix. It hit a raw nerve – went right to the jugular of folks who were paid to be professional voyeurs – in screening rooms. (Stein, *Film Comment*, Sept/Oct 1979)

Stein puts his finger on the fact that a horror film located in our own environment rather than a fantasy setting will always be more threatening to the viewer (as I discuss in more detail elsewhere in this book).

The way in which Powell created the mise-en-scène of *Peeping Tom* underlines his commitment to representing the truth (as defined in The Archers manifesto). In *Peeping Tom* he tried to make the locations that were not part of his own experience (the porn studio, the prostitute's room) as realistic as possible.

Fig 8 The opening sequence, filmed with a predatory hand-held camera in Newman Passage, London. This gripping sequence forces the viewer to share the killer's point of view as the prostitute leads us from the street up to her room, where she will die. © StudioCanal.

The opening scene, so shocking and life-like, was shot in and around Newman Passage in Fitzrovia. At that time, it marked the edge of London's real 'red light district'. Like so many other aspects of the film, Powell chose the location not only because of its physical characteristics, but because of what it was in real life:

> There is a narrow, arched passage – Newman Passage – leading through to Newman
> Street, that gives you gooseflesh just to look at it: they say it is associated with Jack the
> Ripper. (In Christie & Moor, 2019: 144)

Pamela Green, who played the character Milly, was in real life a very successful 'glamour'
(porn) model. She revealed that Powell used and recreated her own existing costumes
and sets for the scenes set in a porn photography studio. In visiting her at her studio she
remembers that:

> Powell was fascinated by the set, he walked around admiring the old street lamp
> and French posters. I had even planted tiny ferns and moss to give it a touch of
> authenticity. He asked if he could copy the set for the film. In the corner of our studio
> was a small set up, consisting of an attic interior with a black iron bedstead with bed
> linen and pillows and various props hanging on the wall. This Powell felt he could use
> for the last scene. We were also to advise him on the lamps and cameras that Mark
> would use. (https://pamela-green.com/essays/filming-peeping-tom/)

For the parts of the film that overlap with his own experience, in and around Mark's
house and the film studio, Powell uses locations that are true to his own life –
autobiographical spaces. Mark's house was actually 5 Melbury Road, Holland Park, while
Powell lived at number 8. Powell filmed the home movies of young Mark using his
son Columba in their own garden and house, and even the studio-shot scenes were
filmed in a small studio local to his home. All of the locations, whether real or created
in a studio, are meant to be as close to reality as possible (even if they are then lit in a
theatrical rather than naturalistic style).

There are details in the film which would have been completely invisible to the audience
but underline Powell's wish to add an autobiographical element to the mise-en-scène.
The cameras set out on shelves in Mark's studio include Powell's own first camera.
Mrs Stephens wears a cardigan owned by Powell's then-wife Frankie, and Mark
wears a jacket which belonged to Powell. It is possible these items were used to cut
costume budgets but it is just as likely Powell included them as a sort of embedded
autobiographical directorial signature.

For the studio scenes Powell shot in Pinewood. Another meta-reference, because he

Fig 9 Maxine Audley as Mrs Stephens, wearing Frankie Powell's cardigan. © StudioCanal.

uses Pinewood as the location for scenes that specifically parody Pinewood – or, more particularly, the workings of the Rank Organisation, which owned Pinewood and made the types of films Powell is making fun of. The director of the film being shot in these studio scenes is called Arthur Baden, another sneaky autobiographical detail as the name derives from Arthur Baden *Powell* (an eminent twentieth-century naturalist). Powell makes the studio the setting for its own take down and even uses many of the regular Pinewood studio crew (for example, his make-up man Bill Partleton was head of make-up at Pinewood).

Although Powell did not intentionally approach his film in the same way as the emerging 'New Wave' of European directors, his own way to choosing sets and locations for the film echoes their cinéma vérité methods. Powell chooses locations that are imbued with significance to the story (autobiographical spaces and real locations) rather than fake fictional spaces, and in doing so adds to the emotional impact of the film on an audience used to seeing horror played out on a reassuringly fake set.

FOOTNOTES

3. https://www.bbfc.co.uk/case-studies/peeping-tom
4. *Peeping Tom* script reproduced at http://www.dailyscript.com/scripts/peepingtom.html

CHAPTER 3: *PEEPING TOM* AS A PROTO-SLASHER

In a short, somewhat flippant article published in *The Washington Post* in 1999, Stephen Hunter identifies *Peeping Tom* as a 'proto-slasher'. He writes that, 'the slasher film itself may have begun here, not in *Psycho* as so many believe, for the film again and again recreates the queasy thrill of the stalk and the power of the kill from the point of view of the murderer, looking through a camera lens' (12 March 1999).

In the late 1970s and through the 1980s slashers emerged as a clearly defined sub-genre of horror. Films categorised as slashers tend to share a set of characteristics that include: a suburban domestic setting; a female teenage heroine; a male killer who suffered a traumatic event or events in childhood; a phallic weapon (often a type of blade); and a series of sketchily portrayed young victims identified for their promiscuity. In the typical slasher, the female heroine defeats the killer at the end of the film but the death of the killer remains ambiguous enough to allow for potential sequels. Technical characteristics include the use of low lighting, dramatic soundtracks, but most importantly the now infamous 'killer's point-of-view' shot.

At a glance, it is easy to see that *Peeping Tom* does share some of these key elements, but is it fair to go further, as some film critics and theorists have, and identify *Peeping Tom* as a proto-slasher?

PEEPING TOM'S USE OF THE POINT-OF-VIEW SHOT

Peeping Tom is highly unusual in that one of the key reasons for its critical mauling was the use of a specific innovative and unusual camera shot generally known as a subjective point-of-view (POV) shot. As Laura Mulvey comments (about *Peeping Tom*), 'The cinema spectator's own voyeurism is made shockingly obvious and even more shockingly, the spectator identifies with the perverted protagonist'.[5]

The POV is a camera shot that has subsequently become synonymous with the slasher sub-genre of horror, to the extent that now it is often seen as a cliché and parodied. In his 2011 book *Going to Pieces: the rise and fall of the slasher film, 1978-1986*, Adam Rockoff gives us an explanation of this shot in the context of the slasher:

One of the most controversial and misunderstood formal aspects of the slasher film is its persistent use of the subjective camera. There are numerous stylistic techniques used to designate subjectivity: a hand-held or shaky camera; an uneasy tracking shot; strange, awkward or unnatural camera angles. […] An absence of reaction shots – employed mainly to hide the killer's identity – also functions to preserve subjectivity and suspense. The prevailing theory states that a subjective camera, by its very nature, represents the point of view of something. In the case of the slasher film, that something is the killer, thereby making the audience vicarious participants in the murders and forcing them to identify with the villain, not the victim. This defines an uneasy and uncomfortable relationship between the audience – who has been conditioned to always root for the hero – and the killer, whose 'view' they are adopting. (Rockoff, 2011: 15)

At the time Powell used it in *Peeping Tom*, this camera viewpoint had only been used experimentally in a very small number of films. An early example of the subjective POV shot can be found in the 1931 Rouben Mamoulian version of *Dr. Jekyll and Mr. Hyde*. Here we abandon the usual (objective) camera viewpoint to instead *become* Jekyll/Hyde, using a camera view that makes us believe we are seeing things through his eyes. Understanding how and why contemporary viewers reacted to Powell's use of this shot in 1960 is key in understanding their reaction to the film itself.

Talking about Powell's decision to use this shot, Thelma Schoonmaker comments:

Michael's startling filmmaking in *Peeping Tom* is really stunning, particularly when you see how different the film is from the Archers' films. The idea of making the main character an aspiring filmmaker was daring. The potentially destructive nature of filmmaking is the theme of the film, really – a fascinating conception. So, to make the camera the eye for the main character seems a natural idea. (Correspondence with the author)

In order to understand why this shot disturbed the audience in the way it did, we need to know more about how the subjective POV differs from more conventional camera viewpoints. By the time *Peeping Tom* was made in 1959/60 the rules of conventional camera technique in Western film had been long established, mainly by the mainstream Hollywood tradition. In fact, the portions of *Peeping Tom* that do not involve a murder demonstrate these conventions very nicely.

Camera shots are combined with editing to convey information about a scene to the audience. The classic structure aims to give the audience as much information as possible about what is going on – it includes establishing wide angle-views of the setting (whether on location or on a studio set) and often a 'shot/reverse-shot' structure for dialogue between two or more characters. The audience typically enjoys a point of view that is superior (we can see more and have more knowledge than the individual characters within the film), and our viewpoint places us outside of the 'world' or fictional space of the film.

With a classic Hollywood approach, we look on passively, without participation in the action, like gods observing from afar. Laura Mulvey wrote in 'Visual Pleasure and Narrative Cinema' that 'The mass of mainstream film, and the conventions within which it has consciously evolved, portray a hermetically sealed world which unwinds magically, indifferent to the presence of the audience, producing for them a sense of separation and playing on their voyeuristic phantasy' (Mulvey, 1989:17).

This 'God's eye view' is supported by camera angles that may give us a viewpoint that could not physically belong to a person/character inside the filmic space – for example, looking down from the ceiling in this shot from *Psycho* (Fig 10). In this shot we are given a privileged point of view that shows us the action but does not (and could not) belong to a character within the film itself.

Fig 10 An impossible shot from the ceiling, at a key moment in Psycho. © Universal.

Fig 11a If we compare this shot to the one taken from Halloween (below Fig 11b), we can see in the difference between the arm placements that the Halloween shot makes us into the owners of the view, whereas the Psycho shot is aligned differently so that we stand beside Lila (as invisible onlookers), rather than becoming her. © Universal.

Fig 11b © Falcon International.

Above all, conventional camerawork aims to be invisible. The camera's job is to show the viewer the action – the viewer should watch the film without their attention being drawn to the presence of the camera itself. This is a vital part of constructing the audience's suspension of disbelief.

As viewers, even if we are encouraged to empathise with a particular character, we rarely share their literal view of a scene. We do not see exactly what they see, but instead inhabit a space just behind them – as demonstrated by Fig 11a, a shot from *Psycho*, which shows us 'Mother' as just discovered by Lila Crane.

Anything outside the conventional way of presenting the action is usually done to create an effect and to initiate a particular emotional response from the viewer. When the audience does share the view of a character, seeing action as if through their eyes, that is done expressly so that we closely identify with the experiences of that character. For example, in an important scene in Hitchcock's *Rear Window* (1954), by sharing L.B. Jeffries' view of the action we share his sense of frustration as he sees his girlfriend Lisa in an increasingly dangerous situation but is unable to help her.

Fig 12 In this shot from Rear Window, *we can see L.B.'s view of the killer. We know we are sharing his actual view because the 'peephole' style tells us we are looking through his camera lens.* © Universal.

The subjective POV shot makes the audience literally look through the eyes of a character. It is generally marked out from ordinary viewpoints by being hand-held rather than shot on a conventional dolly. This means instead of getting a smooth shot, what we see moves as if the 'person' whose view we share is walking along. The shot draws attention to itself, it disrupts our suspension of disbelief.

There is also a point of technical difference between *Peeping Tom* and later slashers. At the time *Peeping Tom* was made the camera could be mounted (on a dolly) or hand held, but the systems most commonly used to create smooth POV shots now, such as the Panaglide or the Steadicam, had not yet been invented.

In *Peeping Tom* Michael Powell's use of this unusual shot in the opening of the film is disorienting. The score is aligned with Mark from this opening shot, when the guitar twang coincides with the opening of his eye (Powell removed frames from the shot so the eye opens quicker than it naturally should). By going from an image of an eye straight into a subjective point of view without using any kind of establishing shot first, Powell temporarily conceals the identity of the character whose disturbing actions we are not only witnessing, but somehow feel implicated in. Even though the very first shot of the film is an extreme close-up of an eye, this eye also reveals nothing about the identity of the person whose eye it is.

The unusual viewpoint spikes our curiosity and draws us in, but also adds a sense of unease because a vital piece of information – 'who is this?' or even 'who am I?' – is being withheld. We know the view we are seeing belongs to an unseen person because it mimics the movement of a person's eye. In a particularly predatory shot the camera even looks the prostitute up and down before following her.

We find ourselves yearning for a mirror reflection glimpse or the 'return' of the 'shot/reverse-shot' which Hollywood convention has primed us to expect. By withholding the identity of the killer Powell creates suspense and tension right from the very beginning of the film. Mark as the owner of the view is not identified till nearly five mins into the film.

In 'Beauty Bests the Beast', Robin Wood notes that the subjective point-of-view camera adds '[t]he sense of indeterminate, unidentified, possibly supernatural or superhuman.

Menace feeds the spectator's fantasy of power, facilitating a direct spectator-camera identification by keeping the intermediary character, while signified to be present, as vaguely defined as possible' (Wood, 1983: 63).

If we again look back at the history of film, in 1960 the audience would expect to be guided towards sympathy with the victim in a horror film. They would identify themselves with the victim or hero/heroine but never the killer. If *Peeping Tom* had followed established conventions Mark would have been clearly defined as a villain and we would have viewed the action from Helen's point of view, as the most obvious 'good' central character.

By physically making the viewer share Mark's point of view Powell forced identification and sympathy with the killer, which made the contemporary viewer extremely uncomfortable. By sharing his view via the subjective point of view shot, we feel implicated in the crimes Mark commits. We recognise Mark's sickness as voyeurism while simultaneously realising that we too are voyeurs. Years after the film was reappraised, Roger Ebert wrote (in 1999), 'Why did critics and the public hate it so? I think because it didn't allow the audience to lurk anonymously in the dark, but implicated us in the voyeurism of the title character' (rogerebert.com).

A natural, though controversial extension of this idea is that by sharing the killer's view, and empathising with the killer, we as audience members could potentially be inspired to act out violent acts in the real world. This was hinted at in some of the *Peeping Tom* reviews, and in the 1980s would become the basis of the 'video nasties' debate in Britain around the perceived harmful influence of horror film videos. Just as *Peeping Tom* is now thought of very differently to how it was received in 1960, many of the films once categorised as 'video nasties' have now obtained certification uncut or with minimal edits. The idea that viewers can be influenced by the films they watch has been inconclusively re-examined in relation to several high-profile real-life murder cases, with journalists often asserting a link between horror films that murderers supposedly watched before carrying out crimes in the face of academic studies that conclude no such thing.

If we look at *Peeping Tom* in relation to the development of the horror genre, the use of the killer's POV sets it apart from contemporary horror films, which were gory and sexy but shot very conventionally. If we look at the film on purely aesthetic terms, the camera work means that *Peeping Tom* does bear a far closer resemblance to the slashers of the 1980s than to other horror films being made in 1960. The opening scenes of *Peeping Tom* and *Halloween* (1978) are uncannily alike – they both open with a killer's POV shot that the audience shares, and a delayed reveal to show who this viewpoint belongs to.

After *Peeping Tom*, the repeated use of the killer's POV in the horror films of the 1980s lead to the shot becoming one of several horror tropes which came to be seen as a cliché. It is even parodied in comedies about horror films (for example the *Scary Movie* series [2000-2013]). The killer's POV ironically became impotent – no longer having the power to disturb the audience in the way that was so clearly demonstrated by the reaction of the 1960 viewers of *Peeping Tom*, who had never come across such a thing before.

A NOTE ON THE SETTING

The setting of the film is something I write about in more detail in Chapter 4, but slashers were important because they moved the action out of the gothic landscape and brought horror into our own homes. In the slasher, the location isn't 'a house', but our *home*. In *The Monstrous-Feminine*, Barbara Creed writes: 'In many films the house is initially depicted as a place of refuge. The monster either shelters or the victim seeks safety in a house. Inevitably, the situation is reversed and the house that offered solace ultimately becomes a trap, the place where the monster is destroyed and/or the victim murdered' (Creed, 1993: 56).

American slashers also largely migrated the horror from rural settings made popular by such films as *Deliverance* (1973), *The Texas Chain Saw Massacre* (1974) and *The Hills Have Eyes* (1977) into suburbia with *Halloween*. The people next door were now the killers.

In *Peeping Tom* the site of the house is further complicated by being the childhood home and current home of the killer Mark, but also the current home of Helen (with her mother). It becomes a deeply significant space from an emotional point of view because Mark associates different rooms in the house with his childhood. Helen is living in his mother's old room and Mark uses his father's study as his own screening and editing room.

This brings us to a very obvious point – one of the biggest differences between *Peeping Tom* and the typical slasher is that it is British. The slasher developed as a uniquely American subgenre, populated by American high school victims, a teenage babysitter-type American teenage heroine, and set in the American suburban home. Slashers explore and exploit American fears and desires. *Peeping Tom* was certainly different from contemporary British horror in that it was set in the real streets and suburbs of London, but from a broader cultural point of view its setting it is vastly different from the 'Middle America' referenced in the slasher.

THE SLASHER AS A YOUTH GENRE

Horror has always been a popular with a younger audience – and this is particularly marked with the slasher, a sub-genre about teens, watched by teens. *Peeping Tom* was made at a point when the power to change British culture was just beginning to move away from the adults of the Second World War generation to the teenage baby boomers. Their impact would later become so important in shaping a new Britain.

Later in the 1960s, changes in film production and exhibition were led by the importance of the youth audience, but in 1960 Powell had accidentally created a film that would appeal to a teen audience that had not yet fully materialised. Helen and Mark might be slightly older than the teen cast of the typical slasher, but the film's focus on the actions and experiences of young people rather than the older adults in positions of power and responsibility does link *Peeping Tom* to the slasher genre.

HELEN AS *PEEPING TOM*'S 'FINAL GIRL'

In her book *Men, Women and Chainsaws* (1992; revised 2015), Carol Clover coined the phrase 'the Final Girl' to describe the female protagonist of the slasher, who, despite all the odds, manages to out-live her teenage contemporaries and eliminate the killer, often with his own weapon.

While *Peeping Tom*'s Helen does not completely match the later stereotype, she certainly has enough Final Girl characteristics to draw some comparison. Like the archetypal Final Girls, she emerges as a female character very different from the female victims of the killer. She is the wholesome 'girl next door'. She is not naïve or stupid, but she is seen as an innocent young woman, especially if we compare her to the other women in the film, the porn models, sex workers, actresses and even her own cynical and alcoholic mother.

According to Clover,

> The Final Girl is boyish, in a word. Just as the killer is not fully masculine, she is not fully feminine – not, in any case, feminine in the ways of her friends. Her smartness, gravity, competence in mechanical and other practical matters, and sexual reluctance set her apart from the other girls and ally her, ironically, with the very boys she fears or rejects, not to speak of the killer himself. (2015: 40)

Many characteristics that Clover mentions are not identifiable in Helen, but she is certainly seen as serious, smart, inquisitive and different from other women portrayed in the film. It is precisely Helen's innocence and purity which attracts Mark to her and ultimately protects her from being killed by him.

According to Clover, the Final Girl is also the 'investigating consciousness' (ibid.) of the film. She is intelligent and curious, and from a plot point of view drives the narrative forwards. This is definitely true of Helen. While we are initially forced to see the action through Mark's eyes, it is Helen's curiosity which drives us towards the film's sad conclusion. As an audience we know more than her, but we still follow Helen as she unfolds the mystery surrounding Mark.

Writing about the slasher in his book on the horror genre, Mark Jancovich mentions that 'It is masculinity, not femininity, that is the problem in these films; and this problem is registered in a number of ways. They display an absence of positive or effective male characters. It is the female heroes who engage the killer...' (Jancovich, 1992: 107). This is certainly true of *Peeping Tom*. Powell portrays the police as almost laughably ineffective, while Helen investigates Mark with intelligence and curiosity.

But where *Peeping Tom* differs from the typical slasher is in its concluding scene. Helen does indeed survive, but it is not as a result of turning on and killing Mark. Her sympathy for him motivates her actions and this is not true of the Final Girl who is motivated by fear and the need to survive. Unlike a typical slasher killer, who nearly always live to kill again in the sequel, there is no chance that Mark will be resurrected.

MARK AS A KILLER

As will be discussed in Chapter 4, Mark has plenty in common with *Psycho*'s Norman Bates, but is a far more complex and fleshed out character than the typical killer in the later slashers. While they share Mark's traumatic childhood and perverted urge to kill, these later characters are often barely more than cyphers, with little or no dialogue, a disguise of some kind and a backstory that only emerges later – we never care for these killers in the way that Powell entreats us to care about Mark. If we think about how the POV shot is used, in *Peeping Tom* it is used to emotionally link us to Mark, but in *Halloween* it is used to obscure the identity of the killer but never adds any level of emotional or psychological depth to Michael Myers.

The character of Mark is not closely identifiable with the killers in 1980s slasher films, but like Helen he does share some characteristics with other film killers. Carol Clover writes that, 'Nor is the gender of the principals as straightforward as it first seems. The killer's phallic purpose, as he thrusts his drill or knife into the trembling bodies of young women, is unmistakable. At the same time, however, his masculinity is severely qualified: he ranges from the virginal or sexually inert to the transvestite or transsexual' (2015: 47).

Mark is subtly portrayed as having an atypical sexual drive – he clearly likes Helen but does not want to (or is afraid to) have a sexual relationship with her, because for him sexualised women are potential victims. He avoids physical intimacy with Helen but caresses his camera in a sexual way. His choice of weapon also links him to the killers in the slasher films Clover writes about (and *Psycho*) – the tripod leg mounted with a blade could be interpreted (in the context of modern feminist theory) as having phallic connotations and the manner of death ('penetration' by this improvised blade) is also sexualised.

In terms of male gender definitions, 1959/60 was at a transitional point between the hypermasculinity of the war hero and the androgynous effeminate pop hero that would lead the way by the end of the decade. Mark represents a generation of men too young to have fought in the Second World War. Young men in the 1960s had to redefine what it was to be a man and Mark reflects that change.

Mark's death at the end of the film confirms his ambiguity from a gender point of view. He is the only male victim – maybe this could be read as Mark never having fully become a man, but remaining (sexually stunted) as a grown version of the young boy his father abused. In the slasher the male killer is often perceived as being not a 'real' man – in other words, not a sexually active heterosexual man. Instead the killer is a man-boy – often trapped in an infantile state as a result of an abusive parent.

This could be said of both Mark and Norman Bates. Mark's constant re-watching of his father's cinefilms show that he has failed to move forward from the abuse of his childhood but continues to re-live the horror on an almost daily basis. The fact that Mark was the object of his father's gaze (and his father's camera's gaze) as a child means that in terms of feminist film theory, Mark is associated with a female trait. His death has a narcissistic element in that he becomes the subject of his own gaze – and this also disrupts the rules of gender as already established. Mark is both the male killer but also the (previously female) victim. By turning his camera on himself, by choosing to be looked at rather than to look, Mark becomes in this context a female victim rather than a male killer. The film really pushes this idea by having Mark penetrating himself with his phallic weapon.

PEEPING TOM, PSYCHOANALYSIS AND THE WRITINGS OF CLOVER, MULVEY AND KRISTEVA

In the 1970s, '80s and into the '90s, feminist film theorists wrote about gender in cinema and in doing so discussed many ideas that are very relevant in relation to Peeping Tom. In particular, Laura Mulvey, Julia Kristeva and Carol Clover all write about gender in relation to horror. But we must remember the context in which they were written while we read these works.

Laura Mulvey's essay 'Visual Pleasure and Narrative Cinema' was written in 1975 at the height of the feminist movement – so while Mulvey's writing is relevant and thought-provoking it does articulate the views of a writer working from a very particular feminist point of view. She says in the opening paragraph that she has a political motivation: 'Psychoanalytic theory, is thus appropriated here as a political weapon, demonstrating the way the unconscious of patriarchal society has structured film form' (1989: 14).

Julia Kristeva's book on abjection was published in 1980, just as Western society (and American society especially) was starting to react against feminism. Clover's *Men, Women and Chainsaws* was published in 1992, which could be regarded as the beginning of the 'post-feminist' period. All three writers are invested in investigating aspects of gender in the horror film. They draw interesting conclusions that highlight similarities between *Peeping Tom* and the slasher but it must be remembered that these are later observations rather than contemporary commentaries. They present a fascinating but very much subjective view of horror given in a completely different cultural context to the one in which Powell made the film.

Laura Mulvey wrote an essay on *Peeping Tom* when it was released on Laserdisc by the Criterion Collection in 1994 (as well as recording a commentary). In it she writes:

> *Peeping Tom*, as its title implies, is overtly about voyeuristic sadism. Its central character is a young cameraman and thus the story of voyeuristic perversion is, equally overtly, set within the film industry and the cinema itself, foregrounding its mechanisms of looking, and the gender divide that separates the secret observer (male) from the object of his gaze (female). The cinema spectator's own voyeurism is made shockingly obvious and even more shockingly, the spectator identifies with the perverted protagonist. It is this relentless exposure of cinematic conventions and assumptions that has attracted the interest of feminist film critics, and the recent application of psychoanalytic theory to film theory clearly reveals the film's psychoanalytic frame of reference.

Freudian psychoanalysis is currently rather out of fashion and the way in which it is used in films such as *Peeping Tom* and *Psycho* can seem crude and even laughable to a twenty-first-century viewer. But we have to suspend our own dismissal of Freudian theory. This is partly because *Peeping Tom* was written (as was *Psycho*) with Freudian theories as a central theme. In *Peeping Tom* Mark's own father is using him to explore psychanalytic theories. Powell and Marks had originally planned to make a film about Freud, so it is not surprising the theme re-emerges in *Peeping Tom*.

Freudian psychoanalytic theory would also be used as a theme in later slashers (for example in another classic of that genre, *A Nightmare on Elm Street* (1984)), and as a result the film theorists who wrote about these films were also interested – so while Freud remains unfashionable in modern approaches to psychology, Freudian psychoanalysis remains an important theme in the horror film and an important starting point from which to write about horror.

In 'Visual Pleasure and Narrative Cinema', Laura Mulvey writes:

> The cinema offers a number of possible pleasures. One is scopophilia. There are circumstances in which looking itself is a source of pleasure, just as, in the reverse formation, there is pleasure in being looked at. [...] He [Freud] associated scopophilia with taking other people as objects, subjecting them to a controlling and curious gaze. His particular examples centre around the voyeuristic activities of children, their desire to see and make sure of the private and the forbidden (curiosity about other people's genital and bodily functions, about the presence or absence of the penis, and, retrospectively, about the primal scene). (1989: 16)

So, in *Peeping Tom*'s film-within-a-film, which shows Mark's father watching Mark who is watching a couple kissing on a bench, Leo Marks and Powell intentionally recreate a text-book example of scopophilia, but by using a point-of-view shot Powell takes this idea even further. Powell makes us watch his killer – confronting and fulfilling the audience's unconscious desire to watch what is forbidden. Powell uses this shot partly to make the audience more sympathetic to Mark, whose gaze they shared, but also in order to shame the audience – to accuse them of sharing the same perversion, scopophilia, as his killer.

ABJECTION – THE LACK OF A BLOODY CORPSE IN *PEEPING TOM*

Julia Kristeva is a French writer whose 1980 work 'Powers of Horror: An Essay on Abjection' gives us another angle both on the slasher, and *Peeping Tom*. Kristeva wrote about abjection in relation to the horror film. She writes that 'abject' refers to the human reaction (horror, vomit, etc.) to a threatened breakdown in meaning caused by the loss of the distinction between subject and object or between self and other.

Her primary example for what causes such a reaction is the corpse. *Psycho* obviously engages with the abject – the blood, the dead eye, the disposal of Marion's body – all of these fulfil Kristeva's description of abjection. This is also true of many slashers, which typically revel in bloody murders and lingering views of penetrating wounds.

Here we have a key difference between the slasher and *Peeping Tom*. *Peeping Tom* shies away from the abject – there is a noticeable lack of blood, we never really see more than glimpses of a corpse – in fact the horror is largely accomplished psychologically. So, if we use Kristeva as a reference, *Psycho* is closer in this respect to a slasher than *Peeping Tom*. However, in *Peeping Tom* we do still get a breakdown of meaning caused by the loss of distinction between self and other. Instead, Powell uses the subjective point-of-view shot to break down the barrier between the viewer and the killer (the 'other'). We identify not with the corpse, but with the killer. There were plenty of more graphic British horror films beginning to be made at this time but Powell avoids that approach.

LAYERS OF MEANING – THE LOOK AND THE GENDERED GAZE

At its most complex, *Peeping Tom* makes the viewer watch Mark, watching Helen's mother, watching victims, watching themselves (die).

Powell takes the theme of voyeurism/scopophilia and explores it to a level that many viewers might never have been aware of. Helen's blind mother is the only person who can 'see' Mark for what he really is. She is also the only person who is truly safe from Mark's murderous intentions because he wants his victims to watch their own death in the mirror mounted on his tripod, and of course as a blind woman she is unable to fulfil this required element of his planned murders.

Mark watches and films the police who are looking for him. The book Helen is writing is about a magic camera. At the studio, Vivian films Mark before he films her – it highlights his own vulnerability and hints at his future as a suicide victim. Powell creates circles and circles around the idea of looking and the potential meanings of different kinds of look.

By casting himself as the father, he creates the film we watch both as the real director of *Peeping Tom* and the fictional 'director' of Mark's childhood films.

In *Men, Women and Chainsaws*, Clover recognises this 'meta' element in *Peeping Tom*, a film about filming: 'It is in any case the self-reflexive dimension of *Peeping Tom* that has led to its revaluation, over the decades, as first and foremost a sustained reflection on the nature of cinematic vision – in the opinion of many the finest metafilm ever made' (2015: 169).

I have already written about the technical point-of-view shot in *Peeping Tom*, and about Mark's somewhat fluid relationship to gender, but feminist writers in the 1970s and later became fascinated with the idea of a 'gendered gaze'.

The study of gendered representations in film began with Molly Haskell's *From Reverence to Rape: The Treatment of Women in the Movies* (1974). The idea was taken on and developed by other (mainly female) writers, especially in relation to the representation of women in horror. Who is watching whom and what does that mean? According to Mulvey:

> In a world ordered by sexual imbalance, pleasure in looking has been split between the active/male and passive/female. The determining male gaze projects its phantasy on to the female figure which is styled accordingly. In their traditional exhibitionist role women are simultaneously looked at and displayed [...]. (1989: 62)

In the simplest terms, Male=killer and Female=victim/potential victim. Mulvey, Clover and others argue that because we share the killer's point of view we (the audience) therefore look at women with an overtly male gendered gaze. In *Peeping Tom*, all of the female victims are very literally 'to be looked at'. The prostitute, the photographic porn model and the actress – their jobs mark them out as existing to be looked at. By comparison, the men look – Mark as a camera man and photographer and killer, the film director, the dirty old man in the newsagents, Mark's father, even the police – they look.

Carol Clover points to the act of photographing specifically as having sadistic undertones in the context of the film: 'the act of photographing is plainly figured as an act of phallic cruelty. Those who are photographed are, with the sole exception of Mark as a child, females (prostitute, actress, models), and the experience of being photographed – of gazing reactively – is figured as an experience of being bruised, scarred, terrified, made to faint, and stabbed to death' (2015: 174).

In the world of *Peeping Tom*, and the world as represented in a typical slasher, the male looks and the female is looked at.

So, can we call *Peeping Tom* a proto-slasher given that it was made in and about a different time, a different culture, and the first recognised slashers were made with little, if any knowledge of it? *Peeping Tom* bears many similarities to slashers but without being a true slasher itself. However, the critical writing which has been done in relation to slashers and '80s horror gives us a new and useful insight into the workings of the film and the reasons for its emotional impact on both the contemporary 1960 audience and the twenty-first-century viewer.

FOOTNOTES

5.   Reproduced at http://www.powell-pressburger.org/Reviews/60_PT/Mulvey.html

CHAPTER 4: A COMPARISON OF *PEEPING TOM* AND *PSYCHO*

On the face of things *Peeping Tom* and *Psycho* could have been expected to have enjoyed a similar reaction from critics. Released the same year, both were made by well-respected and experienced British directors, and both featured softly-spoken killers and violent murders.

But the critical response to the films, and the subsequent audience response was hugely different. Although they acknowledged its violence, the critics allowed Hitchcock his *Psycho* (while not exactly lavishing it with praise) while savaging Powell for *Peeping Tom*. In the US bad reviews from critics did not stop *Psycho* being released and the film was able to pick up via the favourable word-of-mouth audience response, which ultimately lead to it becoming a huge financial success.

In Britain the critics still had great influence and because *Peeping Tom* was pulled from distribution almost as soon as it was released, the film was never given a chance to build up a public following even if the critical reaction was negative.

In this chapter we compare the films themselves and the circumstances in which they were made, to try to better understand the difference in the way the films were received in 1960.

THE DIRECTORS

Hitchcock and Powell had a lot in common. Hitchcock was six years older than Powell, but both men had worked their way up through different roles in the film crew before becoming directors. In his early career (working for Gainsborough Studios in Islington, London), Hitchcock had worked on some German co-productions, working abroad in German studios where he was greatly influenced by the great German Expressionist film-makers, such as FW Murnau.

Powell got his earliest experience of film-making in France, and also worked as a photographer on two early Hitchcock films, *Champagne* (1928) and *Blackmail* (1929), for which he was an uncredited contributor to the script (Lazar, 2003: 30). *Peeping*

Tom and *Psycho* spring from the same inspiration and film heritage. Both Powell and Hitchcock were inspired by and had gained film-making experience in the European cinema of the 1920s and in particular both directors were inspired by Fritz Lang. Lang's film *M*, though different in its details, is a startlingly modern-feeling film about a serial killer. The stalking camera and clever and innovative use of sound (including a leitmotif to identify the killer) are just two stylistic elements that we find in *Peeping Tom*, *Psycho* and later the slasher genre, as discussed in Chapter three.

1939 was a turning point in the career paths of both men. Hitchcock moved to America in that year while Powell signed a contract with Alexander Korda and through him met and began working with Emeric Pressburger, resulting in their Archers creative partnership. But by 1959/60 the two men were at very different stages of their career. Powell had made hugely popular films before, during and after the Second World War with his partner Pressburger, but by 1960 these were well behind him. In 1960 Hitchcock's previous three films were *Rear Window*, *Vertigo (1958)* and *North by Northwest* (1959). His career, boosted by his TV show, spin-off books and self-branding was in considerably better health.

The different positions of power enjoyed by the two directors would make a huge difference to the production and post-production of their films. Hitchcock chose to make *Psycho* as a low-budget film, and was able to finance it himself. When it came to distribution Hitchcock was able to closely control the release of his film. Famously, he asked that late-comers were not admitted to cinemas, because he didn't want the twist of Marion's early demise to be spread to those who had not yet seen the film. In doing so he was manipulating his audience and creating a buzz of controversy and secrecy which would boost publicity for his film.

By 1960 Powell did not have much industry muscle power. He was entirely at the mercy of the finance and distribution companies. He was unable to control how the film was viewed and how it was then publicised (or dropped, as it turns out).

To see the level of pre-release publicity the films got, if we look at the April 1960 issue of the popular British film magazine *Picturegoer*, *Peeping Tom* is not mentioned at all, even though it came out the following month. By comparison, *Psycho*'s leading man Anthony Perkins is on the cover, there is an article inside about Janet Leigh, and *Psycho* itself gets two mentions, even though it did not come out till September of that year.

Fig 13 The publicity for Psycho was tightly managed by Hitchcock in a way that built the word-of-mouth hype that contributed to its success.

Fig 14 In 1960 Tony Perkins was a big star, so Hitchcock's Psycho was already ahead in the publicity stakes.

The way in which the two directors were viewed by critics even before these two films came out was also significantly different. Powell and Pressburger had made films on a wide variety of subjects, and their style was artistic and sometimes (not always) fantastical. The technical brilliance of the cinematography united with quite philosophical themes. Although many of Powell's previous works included dark elements (something that critics of *Peeping Tom* would note), he was not known primarily as a director of thrillers and horror.

Hitchcock had made films across different genres but one of the many reasons the critics may have been kinder to Hitchcock and more forgiving of *Psycho* is that the film was an extension of dark themes Hitchcock was already well known for exploring. By 1960 Hitchcock had deliberately established himself as a brand. A well-loved celebrity in his own right, with his TV programmes and books he had established a sort of tongue-in-cheek naughtiness that meant viewers expected thrills from him, even perversity.

But if Powell had a 'brand' (which is arguable) it was, as one half of The Archers, as a purveyor of a certain type of British (or English) drama – bucolic, even if sometimes sardonic – and he was rather less interested in cultivating a public persona. It is perhaps not a surprise, then, that critics felt betrayed by Powell (as we have seen in the analysis of reviews in Chapter 1), because they did not expect him to make a film that was so different from his previous work.

COMPARING MISE-EN-SCÈNE

It is easy to underestimate how important the difference in setting between the films was when it came to affecting how viewers reacted to the violence of the subject matter. This is particularly true when looking at the difference between the American and British response to the films. *Psycho* begins in the ordinary recognisable world of everyday American life – in a bedroom, on the road in a car, at a motel. But this setting changes after the shower scene to become gradually more gothic – the spooky house, the cellar – these are traditional and instantly recognisable locations for horror films.

Fig 15 Hitchcock starts his film in a generic bedroom, in a modern American city (Phoenix, Arizona) – very different to the traditionally gothic settings of many contemporary horror films. © Universal.

Fig 16 The car marks a transition, from this familiar setting to one which will be more threatening. Marion thinks that she is driving away from trouble, but we know she is driving away from safety and into danger. © Universal.

65

Fig 17 The motel is another place that would be very familiar to an American audience – but not necessarily to a foreign viewer. Filmed at night and in teeming rain, the setting is more visibly threatening. © Universal.

Fig 18 The Bates gothic house. While Hitchcock used an Edward Hopper painting of a real house as the basis for the Bates mansion, the way in which the house is filmed creates the sense of a traditional horror setting (similar to the castles we see in Universal or Hammer horror films). © Universal.

This cultural difference between the two films is perhaps significant. The motel would be an everyday ordinary place for an American viewer, but quite unknown and alien to a British viewer. This lack of familiarity enables the viewer to distance themselves further from the action they are viewing on screen – it makes them feel safer and less threatened. So, for a British viewer *Psycho* was in terms of setting, far less immediate, so perhaps less scary. It did not in any way replicate something that could happen in their own life. Visually *Peeping Tom* has more in common with Hitchcock's 1972 film *Frenzy*. That too was set and shot in real-life London locations.

When Truffaut questioned Hitchcock on the settings in *Psycho*, Hitchcock said:

> The mysterious atmosphere is, to some extent, quite accidental. For instance, the actual locale of the events is in northern California, where that type of house is very common. They're either called 'California Gothic,' or, when they're particularly awful they're called 'California gingerbread.' I did not set out to reconstruct an old-fashioned Universal horror-picture atmosphere. I simply wanted to be accurate, and there is no question but that both the house and the motel are authentic reproductions of the real thing. I chose that house and motel because I realized that if I had taken an ordinary low bungalow the effect wouldn't have been the same. I felt that type of architecture would help the atmosphere of the yarn. (2017: 269)

So, although Hitchcock tries to justify the settings by saying that within the context of the location they are realistic, he does also admit that the gothic house was an ideal fit for the horror plot.

Peeping Tom, on the other hand, encroaches on the ordinary world of its British viewers. Hitchcock relied heavily on sets, because he preferred the ability to fully control the setting. But in *Peeping Tom*, Powell shot partly in real locations. The street where Mark follows his first victim, the porn photography studio and the shop selling dirty photographs, are all real London locations, and we know from the memoirs of Pamela Green that Powell was meticulous in trying to faithfully recreate the studio that she in real life used for porn magazine photo shoots.

Fig 19 Peeping Tom *features real London locations. Here we see Mark on the corner of Percy Street and Rathbone Place, a few minutes' walk from his first victim's flat.* © StudioCanal.

Fig 20 *Powell shot most of his interior shots on sets but he was at pains to faithfully recreate a real London porn studio, which he did with advice from Pamela Green, pictured here.* © StudioCanal.

Like Norman Bates, Mark lives in a large old house. But whereas Norman's is set alone on a hill, like Dracula's castle, Mark's house is in an ordinary street. It has been sub-divided into flats.

Fig 21 Although the house in Peeping Tom *is large and old, it is not gothic and empty, but filled with ordinary people living in flats. Mark's own flat is the only part of the house which has remained unchanged since his childhood.* © StudioCanal.

The house which Powell used as Mark's was in fact just down the road from his own home. Houses of that type were, and are common – to a British viewer very far from the Edward Hopper gothic fantasy of the *Psycho* house. Powell does not grant his audience the detachment from reality which might render the violence of the film impotent – his horror unfolds in a familiar setting (much as many later slashers would be set in ordinary suburban homes). London street locations would become a key element of many later '60s British films (*The Knack, Blow Up*, etc.) and *Peeping Tom* anticipates that cinematic escape from the antiseptic perfection of the studio set.

From purely a set design point of view *Psycho* today looks old fashioned compared to *Peeping Tom*, which has a slightly cinéma vérité and gritty feel to it thanks to the use of real locations as well as Powell's hand-held camera. Hitchcock designed for effect, but Powell seems to have wanted his film to look like real life.

KILLERS AND VICTIMS

How does Mark Lewis compare with Norman Bates? On a superficial level, they are quite alike. Good-looking, gently spoken 'nice young men' that any mother would approve of. Both characters are dramatically different to the types of killers portrayed in most horrors or thrillers of the period. They are not monsters, they are not freaks, they are not foreigners, or historical characters from the past. They are clean-cut young men who appear harmless, 'normal'.

Fig 22 Mark is portrayed as a very normal-looking young man, his youth emphasised by his scooter and duffle coat. Unlike Norman, Mark's appearance does not change throughout the development of the plot. © StudioCanal.

But in both films, we learn that the killer has been damaged by the mistreatment they have suffered under the hands of a parent – in Norman's case his overbearing mother, in Mark's his scientist father. They have become voyeurs – a perversion that both directors identified as interesting to explore because of the position of the viewer as a voyeur. In talking to Truffaut about the opening of *Psycho*, Hitchcock said that opening with the scene between Marion and her lover 'allows the viewer to become a Peeping Tom' (Truffaut, 2017: 266).

So although the film is far less explicitly concerned with the theme, Hitchcock still had the idea of voyeurism woven in to the presentation of his story, and explicitly implies that the audience shares the voyeuristic instincts of the killer.

Both Mark and Norman, in having their psychological problems explained to the audience in a clear way, are to some extent exonerated of their crimes. We see them as men who are acting monstrously because they have been abused. However, the directors manipulate their audiences into feeling sympathy for their killers at different points in the two films. Norman is presented to the viewer as a broadly sympathetic character from early on in *Psycho*; we don't learn the true extent of his abusive relationship with his mother, and subsequent psychosis, until later in the film.

Powell shows his viewer early on in *Peeping Tom* that Mark has been abused, and that his instinct to kill is a direct consequence of this abuse. For example, in a key scene of the film, Helen urges Mark to show her one of his films, but he shows her a film of himself as a child. As the film plays out we come to understand it documents one of his father's experiments, recording his son's fearful reactions. Mark, and we as viewers, watches how Helen's face changes as she understands what is happening, and to whom. This is an important point in the film, because by watching his childhood fear Helen, and the viewer, begins to see Mark not just as a murderer and a social inadequate, but as an abused child. Powell uses these films-within-the-film to show us who Mark is and why he is the way he is. This scene builds audience rapport and sympathy with Mark from early on in the narrative.

Psycho presents 'Mother', through Norman's eyes as a grotesque – almost a mythic caricature. In *Peeping Tom*, Mark's father is seen in film clips and although his behaviour is cruel, he is a real, living man. While there are moments that imply a supernatural element in *Psycho*, before we understand who/what 'Mother' is, that is never the case with *Peeping Tom*.

There is a child-like innocence to both men. Both Norman and Mark could be described as suffering from arrested development – forever unable to fully become adults due to the shadow of childhood abuse. These two male leads are interesting in terms of masculinity, or rather, their lack of it. In common with so many slasher villains in later years, both men vent their sexual suppression by killing their victims with phallic weapons. The implication is that they penetrate women with blades because they are unable to bring themselves to have conventional sex.

Norman is child-like and asexual – his only involvement with women (other than 'Mother') seems to be in spying on then killing Marion. Norman initially comes across as boyish and awkward, especially compared to the sexually confident, worldly Marion. But by the end of the film he has become grotesque, a pantomime figure, mad and dressed in his mother's clothing. To some extent you could argue that while *Psycho* initially sets out to be modern and innovative, by the end of the film it has largely returned to a familiar horror setting and scenario. Audiences would find Norman's madness comforting because in the end he is as different to us as the usual horror film monsters.

Fig 23 At the end of Psycho *Norman has transformed from the innocent boyish man we see at the start of the film to someone who is clearly mad.* © Universal.

In *Peeping Tom*, Mark is also portrayed with a boyish innocence, even though (unlike Norman, as far as we know) he is a serial killer. His youth is emphasised by his costume, including a duffle coat one might associate with a school boy. Because Powell interweaves 'film-within-film' scenes of Mark as a child, and indeed Mark's last dialogue is spoken in his child voice, we never lose the impression of Mark-as-child.

Norman is physically removed from the ordinary everyday world but Mark is not only living and working in the city, he is working around the fringes of the sex trade. But, while Mark photographs women for 'under the counter' porn pics, he keeps his distance. When he photographs Lorraine, the model with the hare lip, he says 'you needn't be shy of me…it's my first time too'. He looks out of place in the porn photo studios he sometimes works in, something Milly teases him about.

Mark does not undergo Norman's transformation into a grotesque figure (Mother) – there is no fancy dress, and while he is undoubtedly mentally ill there is no obvious descent into madness, no secondary personality to escape into. Mark remains a damaged young man – a character that Powell urges us to sympathise with, but whose violence he does not fully justify with melodramatic insanity.

Peeping Tom implicates the viewer, the British film establishment (both producers and critics) and hypocritical society, but it never criticises Mark. Instead he is seen as an innocent whose perversion is a direct result of his upbringing, and to a lesser extent the society in which he lives.

The way in which Norman and Mark kill shows that although they have much in common as men they are very different murderers. Norman's frenzied attack is portrayed as an act of passion rather than something premeditated by a cold killer. Norman may have other victims but we never see them.

Mark is shown as a serial killer, carrying out a series of murders that all conform to the same pattern as he tries to film the perfect moment of fear. He approaches this in an almost scientific way (as he would have seen from his father's work) and his victims are, to him, largely meaningless, merely specimens in his experiment.

This difference between Norman and Mark is also emphasised by the way they act after they murder. Norman, returning from his 'Mother' episode, is shocked by the mess and

Hitchcock treats us to a long scene of Norman cleaning up and disposing of the body. Norman is upset by what he sees and tries to remove any trace of the murder. Mark makes no attempt to clean up or conceal his murder scenes. He simply walks away. Norman is desperate to cover up his crime but Mark is almost willing the police to find him. He returns to the scenes of his crimes, like an arsonist watching his own fire.

CASTING

In terms of casting, *Psycho* and *Peeping Tom* were quite different. *Psycho* starred well-known Hollywood stars in all the key roles. *Peeping Tom* had a few well-known actors in smaller parts (including Moira Shearer) but the two central roles, Mark and Helen, were cast with relatively unknown actors (although Böehm was well-known to a European audience). This is significant because it has an impact on the ability of the audience to suspend their disbelief. Mark Lewis may well have been a more unnerving character to watch because most viewers were able to forget he was played by an actor and fully immerse themselves in the fictional space of the film. However wonderful Anthony Perkins' performance as Norman Bates is, most viewers would have known him quite well from other films and the showbiz publicity campaigns he regularly featured in. They would have watched the film with a background familiarity with the actor that would disrupt their ability to believe that Norman Bates is real.

Helen and Marion

As we have seen, the killers Norman and Mark do have some things in common. This is not true of the female leads Marion and Helen, who are quite different. Hitchcock and Powell cast their actresses carefully to emphasise certain points about the characters they were playing.

If we look at them in relation to modern slasher films we can see that they conform to two different genre stereotypes. Marion is first seen getting dressed after sex in a hotel room. She is beautiful, sexually active and in control – a modern woman (who also has something to hide). Both the theft of money and the affair she is having make her morally ambiguous. In the context of the tropes established by later slasher films, she's destined to die as the first victim precisely because of the corruption she represents.

Fig 24 Our very first view of Marion is in bed, and then kissing her lover, wearing only underwear.
© Universal.

Helen, on the other hand, is an early version of Clover's 'Final Girl'. This character is seen as innocent and not (explicitly at any rate) sexually active, inquisitive but not worldly.

Fig 25 Helen celebrating her 21st birthday party. © StudioCanal.

As Helen's curiosity pushes her to find out more about Mark she is something like the Goldilocks or Red Riding Hood female characters found in fairy tales. Although Powell and Hitchcock made their films 20 years before the slasher became a recognised sub-genre, if we approach these films as slashers it is *inevitable* that Marion dies but Helen survives. Helen is the only woman Mark wants to protect from his own dark urges. It is always sexual innocence which invisibly protects the Final Girl.

You could argue that Helen's girlishness leads to a lack of complexity when you compare the character to the short-lived Marion. In some ways Helen's mother, blind and alcoholic, is the more interesting and intriguing character.

Again, the casting of these characters was key. Janet Leigh was 10 years older than Anna Massey. Marion comes across as maybe only a little older than Norman, but very much more worldly. By comparison, although we see Helen celebrate her 21st birthday, at times Mark and Helen act almost like teenagers in love rather than adults. Anna Massey was just beginning her film career (and would have been unfamiliar to viewers), while Janet Leigh was a full-blown Hollywood movie star.

Other victims

One of the key plot differences between *Peeping Tom* and *Psycho* is that one film revolves around the dramatic murder of a single key character (although a subsequent murder take place) while the other features a series of lower impact murders, starting with the death of an almost anonymous prostitute. In *Peeping Tom* women are all potentially expendable. Mark's victims are, like Marion, marked out by their sexual promiscuity, explicitly so with sex workers and porn models Dora and Milly, but even Vivian's job as an actress is one historically associated with 'loose women' of easy morals. Vivian is played by Moira Shearer, the best-known actor in the whole film. The anonymity of the other victims is compounded by the fact that the actresses who played them (just the same as the actors in the lead roles) were not especially well-known at the time.

CINEMATOGRAPHY

Both Hitchcock and Powell were what could be described as technical directors as well as artistic visionaries. What is meant by this is that they understood how every element of the film-making process comes together and both men were involved in everything from deciding which lens was needed for a shot, to being heavily involved in steering costume choice, set design, sound, lighting and editing. Hitchcock was interviewed extensively about the making of *Pyscho*. When Truffaut asked him 'Would you say that *Psycho* is an experimental film?', Hitchcock's response shows clearly the type of director he believed himself to be:

> Possibly. My main satisfaction is that the film had an effect on the audiences, and I consider that very important. I don't care about the subject matter; I don't care about the acting; but I do care about the pieces of film and the photography and the sound track and all of the technical ingredients that made the audience scream. I feel it's tremendously satisfying for us to be able to use the cinematic art to achieve something of a mass emotion. And with *Psycho* we most definitely achieved this. It wasn't a message that stirred the audience, nor was it a great performance or their enjoyment of the novel. They were aroused by pure film. […] That's why I take pride in the fact that *Psycho*, more than any of my other pictures, is a film that belongs to film-makers, to you and me. (Truffaut, 2017: 282-3)

Powell's mentions of *Peeping Tom* in his memoirs are less detailed, but Pamela Green wrote memoirs in which she mentions Powell's involvement in key set design, lighting and costume decisions relating to her character.

In *Psycho* and *Peeping Tom*, the cinematography was achieved as a collaboration between the directors and the camera technicians. In understanding the contemporary response to these films one very obvious difference stands out. *Peeping Tom* is shot in colour while *Psycho* is black and white. 1960 was a cross-over period when films were being shot in either format. However, the three films Hitchcock had shot leading up to *Psycho* were all in colour, so why did he take what could be seen as a retrograde step? He chose to shoot *Psycho* in black and white for two reasons – it was cheaper (Hitchcock paid for the production himself), but also it enabled him to tone down the impact of Marion's bloody death. In an interview with Charles Thomas Samuels (1972), Hitchcock confirmed this motivation: 'I made *Psycho* in black and white purposely to avoid the blood. Red would have been unpleasant, unnecessary; I wouldn't have been able to treat the blood cinematically, as in the editing of its flow down the drain and so on, had the sequence been in colour' (in Lazar, 2003: 136).

He also told Truffaut, 'It's true I filmed *Psycho* in black and white to avoid showing red blood in the killing of Janet Leigh in the shower scene' (2017: 334).

The decision to shoot in black and white achieved what Hitchcock intended – he was able to show graphic violence but in black and white it was less shocking to watch. It gave the audience a level of detachment from real life, making it less realistic made it less threatening. It was also a visual contrast to the lurid colour palette of most contemporary British and American horror films. *Peeping Tom* is in colour – in fact one could argue that it is in heightened colour. It was shot using Eastmancolor, which at the time was used widely in horror films and to the modern viewer seems particularly lurid. *Peeping Tom* exhibits Powell's trademark theatrically (and not realistic) intense use of colours, especially red and green, a continuation of a style he had developed in his other films – although he did not make *Peeping Tom* with previous collaborator Jack Cardiff, visually this film has much in common with previous Powell colour films, such as *The Red Shoes*.

Fig 26 A theatrically lit street scene at the start of Peeping Tom. *While Powell did use real-life locations, his high-contrast creative lighting, combined with the florid tones of Eastmancolor makes even these look artificial at times.* © StudioCanal.

The critics of *Peeping Tom* found it violent and distasteful but *Psycho* is actually far more graphic in its depiction of violence. In *Psycho* we see the weapon being used more clearly, we see blood, we see a corpse and the body being disposed of. As already discussed, the use of black and white helps the viewer to distance themselves from the violence, but so does Hitchcock's use of particular camera viewpoints.

Hitchcock gives the viewer a 'God's eye' POV that gives us a superior view of the action, encourages us to empathise with the victim, but also allows us a degree of separation – we look on, but we do not take part. At the start of the shower sequence, when Marion is writing at the desk, we do actually have a point-of-view shot – showing her hand writing in the notebook. Hitchcock precedes the violence by making sure the audience is identifying closely with the victim.

The number of different shots in this sequence (and the way they are edited together) is far more complicated than Powell's camera in *Peeping Tom* (and is the subject of a documentary film devoted to it: *78/52: Hitchcock's Shower Scene* (2017)). Hitchcock lends a predatory air to the scene by placing the camera in an impossibly intimate position, inside the shower with Marion, looking at her mainly from the side or from above, but occasionally using single point-of-view shots to underline our (the viewer's) position as sharing the victim's point of view.

Fig 27 In this shot from the shower sequence we can see that Hitchcock has placed the camera inside the shower, to mimic the point of view of the victim. © Universal.

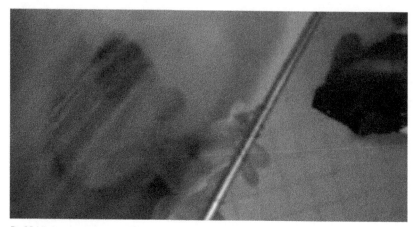

Fig 28 Hitchcock switches to a 'God's eye view', placing the camera outside of the action to give the audience an impossible overview of the scene (the view would have to be on the ceiling), showing both victim and killer. © Universal.

In a later scene in *Psycho* we do see the hand of the killer, but while in *Peeping Tom* the angle implies the hand is 'ours', in *Psycho* the shot is at an angle that means it cannot be 'our' hand.

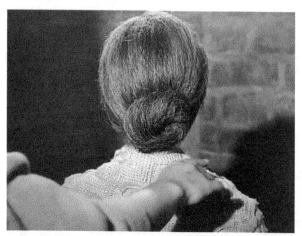

Fig 29 Hitchcock has lined this shot up to show Lila's hand on the shoulder of Mother's skeleton. The angle of the arm tells us that we are standing next to Lila, the arm is hers, not ours. We are not sharing her literal point of view. © Universal.

The difference between the two angles is vital in changing the way the viewer relates to the action shown. Hitchcock sometimes uses camera angles to encourage us to empathise with the victim (as in Figure 31 above, where we share Lila's trepidation in the cellar), but as viewers we remain outside of the action in the safety of our seats.

Jump cuts and zooms in the shower sequence are used cleverly by Hitchcock to mimic the cutting motions of his killer's hand, but the other effect is to draw attention to the artificiality of the camera position, whereas Powell's hand-held camera mimics real life. The fast editing and sheer number of shots per minute contrast with the much slower 'gaze' of Powell's predatory camera. As viewers, we feel far more like voyeurs ourselves in *Peeping Tom*.

Psycho has one important murder scene around which the whole plot hangs (although 'Mother' will later kill private investigator Arbogast). But Mark in *Peeping Tom* is a serial killer. The first murder we witness is, the wider context of the narrative almost irrelevant. Unlike Marion, who we take to be the lead female in *Psycho*, the prostitute who dies in the opening scene of *Peeping Tom* is virtually anonymous. Mark follows Dora along a street and up into her room before murdering her. As discussed in more detail in Chapter 3, this is all shot as a subjective POV shot unbroken for the duration of the murder. The 'set up' shots tell us only that the view we are sharing belongs to an unidentified man:

Just as 'Mother' in *Psycho* is almost a character in 'her' own right, in *Peeping Tom* there are times when Mark's camera seems to have a life of its own. In the opening sequence this is underlined by the fact that (due to the establishing shot that shows the camera being held at chest height rather than to his eye), we actually see what the camera sees rather than what Mark himself sees. Later in the film we see Mark caress and even kiss his camera – he treats it like a lover. The original script layout refers to 'Camera' almost as a role in its own right. By treating the camera in this way Mark to some extent distances himself from the murders he commits (just as Norman does the same by dressing in his mother's clothes to disassociate himself from the crime he is committing). The camera kills the victims – in the act of killing them, Mark often avoids making any physical contact with his victims.

Fig 30 We see a man walking into a street, from the back, in the dark, so his identity is not made clear. He whistles but does not speak (possibly a Powell reference to the whistling killer in Fritz Lang's M). © StudioCanal.

Fig 31 Now we see a close up of a camera, which is being held at waist height by the man. © StudioCanal.

Unlike Hitchcock's shower scene, which includes shots that mimic Marion's point of view, in *Peeping Tom* we exclusively share the sadistic gaze of the killer. As viewers, the camerawork means we feel actively involved in the murder taking place – we are forced to share Mark's view during the murders he is carrying out.

Fig 32 Finally, we see what the camera 'sees', a viewpoint identified by the crosshairs of the lens. We will continue through the scene occupying this view. Seeing a character through cross hairs in Peeping Tom *can signify their status as a victim – interestingly the first time Helen sees Mark he is framed this way, by the window he is looking through.* © StudioCanal.

If we compare the two murder scenes, *Psycho*, with its staccato soundtrack, fast editing and blood feels far more violent. But audiences were more shocked by *Peeping Tom* because the different use of camera angles leads us to feel that in *Psycho* we are the victim, and in *Peeping Tom* we are the killer.

Fig 33 The fact that we are seeing what the unidentified man is seeing is emphasised by the shot which shows his hand come into view to throw the film packet away. The angle of the shot, and the fact the camera looks at the hand, shows us that the hand is 'our' hand. © StudioCanal.

FILM ENDINGS

Psycho becomes more like a conventional horror/thriller as it goes along. Although it begins very unconventionally, with the unexpected and violent death of its central female character, by the end of the film we have a mad killer in a gothic castle with a spooky cellar. The film ends with Norman safely in custody and clearly diagnosed as insane. From a 1960 audience point of view, this is relatively familiar and any loose ends are nicely tied up, albeit in a very unHitchcockian wordy 'explanation' scene.

Peeping Tom is far more ambiguous. It ends with Mark's suicide. Helen's reaction of grief rather than relief signals that we should feel sad that this serial killer has died. It's a more unusual and morally ambiguous ending – Hitchcock ultimately returns to a more conventional story but Powell continues to defy conventions until the very end of his film.

The differences in the films highlight differences in their directors. While Powell made his film to the best of his artistic abilities he also did not shy from making a challenging and sometimes difficult to watch film, hoping that audience members would be drawn into the story and accepting of its killer antihero. But he underestimated how damaging a negative critical response could be. Hitchcock successfully anticipated potential issues and tried to mitigate them. In choosing to film in black and white and constructing the finale of *Psycho* in a more conventional manner, Hitchcock seems to have knowingly catered for what the audience (and the critics) would accept and avoided what they would not. While both men were artistic directors of great talent, Hitchcock seems to have been far more commercially minded when making *Psycho* than Powell was, making *Peeping Tom*.

In an interview with Bill Kelley for *Femme Fatale Magazine* (published in July 1996), Powell remarked, '*Psycho* was tremendous, in every way. I thought, "Well, the Old Master's done it again," because of the humour, and sent him a wire to Hollywood. Next night the phone rang, and I heard the great voice say, "This is Hitchcock calling London. Thank you, old boy."'

CHAPTER 5: *PEEPING TOM*'S LASTING INFLUENCE AND REHABILITATION

Powell described *Peeping Tom* as 'A film to be tasted with delight in the centuries to come' (in Lazar, 2003: 64). Although he failed to anticipate the initial horrified response of critics and the public to his film, after the shock of its failure, Powell was still optimistic that it might become more palatable as time wore on, and as it turned out, he was right.

Peeping Tom is certainly not a perfect film, and many would argue it is far away from the artistic accomplishment of *The Red Shoes* or other earlier Powell films. Indeed, the primary intent of this book is to make the case for its cultural influence rather than its artistic worth. The way Powell uses his lens to expose the voyeurism of the audience was ground-breaking and his meta theme of the obsessive film-maker appeals to the slightly fanatical love film-makers still have for their craft. Film fans and film-makers have reversed the condemnation of the critics to make sure that *Peeping Tom* is celebrated.

The critical 'rehabilitation' of a piece of art which has initially been condemned, is something that has happened throughout history, in relation to all forms of art, but usually to a less dramatic extent than has been the case with *Peeping Tom*. In *Frightmares*, his book about the history of British horror films, Ian Cooper writes: '*Peeping Tom* is … perhaps the most critically lauded film to appear in this book. It's certainly unique in the way responses to it have so dramatically changed, from revulsion and outrage to its recently-acquired (and much deserved) status as modern classic' (2016: 67).

Films criticised for being bad don't usually magically get better over time. But the original critics of *Peeping Tom* did not say it was badly made, only distasteful. In fact, some managed to criticise the moral position of the film while acknowledging that it was well acted and well made. In the longer term what this meant was that as society changed over time, there was an opportunity to reappraise *Peeping Tom*. The cultural climate in which it was first released has changed, and the passing of time allows for a different perspective.

A key figure in the rehabilitation not only of *Peeping Tom*, but ultimately Michael Powell's entire oeuvre, was director Martin Scorsese, who grew up watching The Archers' films on TV and very much admired Powell from an early age. Scorsese said in 2010:

I have always felt that *Peeping Tom* and *8½* say everything that can be said about film-making, about the process of dealing with film, the objectivity and subjectivity of it and the confusion between the two. *8½* captures the glamour and enjoyment of film-making, while *Peeping Tom* shows the aggression of it, how the camera violates… From studying them you can discover everything about people who make films, or at least people who express themselves through films. (Gritten, *The Telegraph*, 27 August 2010)

In 1979, as a newly-successful director himself, Scorsese found he had the money and the industry clout to acquire and re-release *Peeping Tom*. As Thelma Schoonmaker (Scorsese's editor and Powell's second wife) recalls in an interview, 'Marty raced back to America and said, "I've found him, I've found him! Bring him to the Telluride Film Festival, we'll enter *Peeping Tom* in the New York Film Festival", and it was a huge hit there. It was as if a bomb went off. People like Francis Coppola saw it for the first time, and Marty put up his own money to partially fund the re-release of the movie' (unpublished correspondence with the author).

Scorsese met Michael Powell in 1975 and the two had become friends. Scorsese was motivated to re-release the film partly because of this close friendship, but also because of all of the films Powell had been involved in, *Peeping Tom* had a special resonance with Scorsese. Talking in a 2010 interview, he commented that 'It still speaks to me … I am still surprised at times by how disturbingly beautiful it is' (Kermode, 2010).

The appearance of the film in the 1979 New York Film Festival marked a turning point not only in the fortunes of *Peeping Tom*, but of Powell himself, who was rediscovered and once again recognised as an artistically significant director (although arguably this change had already begun with a BFI retrospective of Powell and Pressburger curated by Ian Christie the previous year). Powell and Scorsese really understood and liked each other. Powell was full of praise for his new friend:

This pocket dynamo was to become my mentor. With his own money, he had helped arrange the final finance for a distribution contract in the USA for *Peeping Tom*, after its enthusiastic reception at the New York Film Festival. Throughout Marty had behaved like a friend and more than a friend, a brother. He could never quite believe that the living, breathing Michael Powell was sitting or more likely walking about the room, talking, moving; and I could hardly believe that this gifted porcupine, bristling with likes and dislikes, could really be the Martin Scorsese of *Mean Streets*, *Taxi Driver* and *Raging Bull*. (Powell, 1986: 567)

The change in context – in terms of time and location - for the re-release elevated *Peeping Tom* before anyone had even seen it. Because he was both a film-maker and passionate film fan, Scorsese also had a real understanding of how to relaunch the film. Whereas the general release planned for the UK in 1960 pitched the film as a mainstream thriller/horror, the 1979 re-release transformed it. By being shown at a well-known film festival the film was now re-framed as art. By placing it into a film festival it was seen by film enthusiasts who were far more likely to take it seriously than the original general release intended in 1960. Film festival viewers were more film literate, and more likely to react favourably to something controversial, foreign and artistic. The romantic details of its rediscovery (and that of its director) gave it an element of glamour and intrigue that were obviously missing the first time around. *Peeping Tom* was now a film which had been talked about for years but rarely seen, it had acquired a near mythical status that did it no harm at all on its re-release.

Fig 34 Michael Powell shows his friend Martin Scorsese the Newman Passage location where he shot the opening sequence of Peeping Tom. *Credit: Martin Scorsese Collection, NY.*

The reviews from the 1979 re-release read very differently to the mainly vitriolic reviews of 1960. British (and US) society had changed immeasurably since the film's original release, and this and other factors in turn had changed the way certain aspects of the film were interpreted. In 1960 the British critics had certain expectations of Powell, based on his successful previous films. They watched *Peeping Tom* comparing it to Powell's existing body of work. By 1979 there were no such expectations, Powell having largely disappeared in the intervening decade (in no small part due to the reception of the film). The film was evaluated on its own terms, not in relation to *The Red Shoes*, *The Life and Death of Colonel Blimp* (1943) or *A Matter of Life and Death* (1946), resulting in responses such as, 'If I were forced, at the point of a sharpened tripod leg, to name the ten best films I have ever seen, that list would include *Peeping Tom*' (Johnson, 1980).

In 1960 *Peeping Tom* had stood out for its violent murder scenes. But by 1979 explicit onscreen violence was commonplace. *Halloween* had traumatised audiences in 1978 and *Alien* was released earlier in 1979. The slasher would become the new norm in the horror genre, and audiences more accustomed to the stalking killer's POV camera and graphic violence. In 1979 the public (and the critics) were less shockable, less squeamish, less prudish, and more likely to recognise the skill and artistry behind *Peeping Tom*.

As previously noted, Powell was never keen on *Peeping Tom* being labelled as horror. However, in the US in 1979 that was no longer a potentially damaging categorisation. In the late 1970s and into the '80s the American horror genre was enjoying a golden age of creativity. In the decade just before the re-release, films including *Rosemary's Baby* (1968), *The Exorcist* (1973), *The Omen* (1976) and *Carrie* (1976) transformed the genre and won mainstream critical recognition for a genre previously written off as pulp.

By far the most illuminating later review is one written by Dilys Powell in 1994. In 1960 Powell had been one of the UK's most influential film critics, and the writer of one of *Peeping Tom*'s most negative reviews. In her 1994 *Sunday Times* review Powell criticises her own negative 1960 response to the film and tries to understand how she could have seen *Peeping Tom* so differently on its original release:

> Michael Powell has long been known as one of this country's most distinguished film-makers. But when, in 1960, he made a horror film, I hated the piece and, together with a great many other British critics, said so. Today, I find I am convinced that it is a

masterpiece. If in some afterlife conversation is permitted, I shall think it my duty to seek out Michael Powell and apologise. Something more than a change of taste must exist.

[…] With so gifted a director this can hardly be anything but a frightening movie, but its object is the examination of emotion and not titillation. Interesting that it should be revived now when there has been much concern about the influence of cinema. All the more reason to distinguish between the serious and the merely sensational horror. Reading now what I wrote in 1960 I find that, despite my efforts to express revulsion, nearly everything I said conceals the extraordinary quality of *Peeping Tom*. See it, and spare a moment to respect the camerawork of Otto Heller. (Powell, 1994)

It is interesting to look at the specific elements Dilys Powell reconsiders in her later, apologetic review. By saying 'Something more than a change of taste must exist', she hints that this change is not simply a matter of personal preference, but of context, a cultural shift rather than a purely personal one. The world in 1960 was very different to the world at the time this second evaluation of the film was written.

By saying 'All the more reason to distinguish between the serious and the merely sensational horror', she implies that the original viewers (including herself) failed to do that – perhaps writing the film off because it belonged to a genre they associated with sensationalist trash. Dilys Powell uses this later review to confirm Michael Powell's quality as a director, but also to specifically name Leo Marks and Otto Heller as his co-creators, in the case of the cinematographer a validation of the integral role the camerawork played in eliciting the original reaction to the film.

INFLUENCE

One of the reasons that *Peeping Tom* is now seen as an important film, is that it has directly influenced other film-makers. Apart from the slasher, within the horror genre the Italian *giallo* films, predominantly of the 1960s and '70s, have many stylistic similarities with *Peeping Tom*. The use of unrealistic saturated colours, unusual framing and camerawork and closeups of eyes and knives are very much visible in both *Peeping Tom* and many *giallos*.

Chris Gallant, in his 2001 overview of the films of *giallo* director Dario Argento, writes:

> Little attention has been paid to the enormous influence that *Peeping Tom* exerted
> over the Italian horror film. Many critics have located the genesis of the *giallo* in *Evil*
> *Eye* (1962) and *Blood and Black Lace* (1964), two films by Mario Bava. But while *Evil*
> *Eye* exhibits the hallmarks of Hitchcock's influence, the gruesome and baroque *Blood*
> *and Black Lace* bears striking similarities to *Peeping Tom*, in terms of both directors' use
> of camera movement, colour, lighting and basic story structure. (Gallant, 2001: 12)

Gallant concludes, 'I would assert that both *Peeping Tom*'s visual style and its themes of
spectator/screen relations became absorbed by Italian horror film culture…' (ibid.).

Crediting *Peeping Tom* with a much broader influence on later films, Oscar Goff, writing
for bostonhussle.com, comments that

> *Peeping Tom* is unmistakably present in the five decades of horror that followed: in the
> dreamy, Technicolor nightmares of Dario Argento and Mario Bava; in the button-down
> psychopaths of Bret Easton Ellis and Thomas Harris (*Red Dragon*'s Francis Dolarhyde
> even shares Lewis' home theater set-up); in the found-footage voyeurism of *The Blair*
> *Witch Project* and its progeny. Martin Scorsese is particularly effusive in his praise of
> the film, and it's not hard to see [Mark] Lewis' influence on Travis Bickle or Rupert
> Pupkin. Hell, *Peeping Tom* even anticipates the cultural fear of snuff films, over a decade
> before the term was coined.

Film-makers including Scorsese and Bernard Tavernier have been very vocal thorough
their careers in crediting Powell with having inspired them, with *Peeping Tom* often
identified as a direct influence.

A REHABILITATION TOO FAR?

When a piece of art is first dismissed, then at a later date re-discovered by a new
generation, is it possible that the new positive evaluation can go too far? The rehabilitation
of *Peeping Tom* has indeed been dramatic. It was reviled, but is now routinely included
on 'best of' lists as an example of visionary film-making. Is it fair to see *Peeping Tom* as a
masterpiece, or is that label as extreme as the original 'trash' that critics ascribed to it?

In his 1979 review of the film Vincent Canby commented, 'Only someone madly obsessed with being the first to hail a new auteur, which is always a nice way of calling attention to oneself, could spend the time needed to find genius in the erratic works of Mr. Powell' (*New York Times*, October 1979). Just as the original release had the occasional good review, not every review of the reissue was entirely positive.

Many of the things *Peeping Tom* is now lauded for are incidental rather than intentional, in particular, its reputation as a proto-slasher. Powell himself did not even really see *Peeping Tom* as a horror film, commenting:

> Of course, I don't think of it as just a horror film at all. I tried to go beyond the ordinary horror film of unexplained monsters, and instead show why one human being should behave in this extraordinary way – it's a story of a human being first and foremost. That's why I had my own son play the central character as a child. (*The Thunderer*, 5th July 1960)

It may be that Powell did not knowingly set out to make a film that pushed the horror genre in new directions. But in the history of cinema *Peeping Tom* foreshadowed many techniques that would subsequently become standard approaches in horror, from the predatory hand-held camera to the stylised lighting and insistent musical score. As discussed earlier in Chapter 3, visually the killer's point of view is very close to the viewpoint that John Carpenter created in *Halloween*, but although this is true, it is a coincidence, because Carpenter claims he had not seen *Peeping Tom* at the time he made his own film. The 'meta' aspects of the film would also later become popular as a horror film trope – films about making films.

Peeping Tom was rediscovered and championed by a director (Scorsese) and has been admired by other directors and film school students. Many of those who appreciated it, and Powell's other films, in the 1979 relaunch were film school students or graduates. Powell was embraced by America's famous 'Movie Brats' generation of up-and-coming directors. The 1979 film audience that helped rehabilitate the film's reputation was entirely different to the one it had been made for.

If we look at the subject matter of *Peeping Tom*, a film which Michael Powell admitted at the time is really about directing/film-making, it makes sense that the film appeals more to these viewers, than the film critics who originally completely misunderstood what Powell was trying to say about the obsessive love of film-making. Peeping Tom's themes and cinematic style fit perfectly into the context of 1970s American film-making, which was dominated by directors aspiring to become auteurs – Scorsese, Lucas, De Palma, Spielberg, Coppola, etc.

The reappraisal of Peeping Tom can also be considered to be a key element in the rehabilitation of Michael Powell as a director. Thanks to the American film critic Andrew Sarris, through the 1970s the idea of the auteur developed from its origin in Cahiers du cinema as a theory for analysing a director's body of work to becoming a shorthand for directorial greatness, and as much a marketing concept as an aesthetic one. Whether Powell saw himself as an auteur or not, his film was one which spoke to those directors who emerged at a time when great faith was being put in their talents by the studios. Martin Scorsese put his own money into re-releasing Peeping Tom and championed Powell, who was then given a job by another director-fan, Francis Ford Coppola at his own mini-studio American Zoetrope. He had found his perfect audience.

Two other aspects of the 1979 rerelease are important. Firstly, the location. It is significant that the film finally succeeded in the US. On its initial release in 1960 it was shown in the UK but denied a US release. This change in cultural context meant that various aspects of the film lost their negative impact and potency. As discussed in previous chapters Powell wove many jokes and criticisms of British culture into the film. Snide digs at the prudish middle classes and many more specific digs aimed at the British film industry. These were completely irrelevant when shown to a 1979 American audience, so did not create the same negative impression as they had when shown to an audience of British critics in 1960.

Chapter four's comparison of Peeping Tom with Psycho considers how a horror film impacts on the viewer when it shows horrific events taking place in their own 'space' – so an American viewer might find a slasher set in a recognisably US suburban home particularly scary. Peeping Tom's locations were entirely alien to the 1979 American viewers, so again, this may have somewhat mitigated its visceral, shocking impact.

Another important change to take into consideration is the relative power and influence of the film critic in 1960 Britain versus 1979 New York. In America the enormous size of the cinema-going public has historically meant that while there *are* hugely influential critics, ultimately 'bums on seats' define the financial success of a film, so a positive word-of-mouth reaction can lead to huge success in spite of a negative critical response. In Britain in 1960 the critics had a disproportionate amount of power. The number of cinema-goers was (obviously) far smaller, and the relative power of the critic far greater. Overall the location and date of the re-release provided *Peeping Tom* with a far greater chance of success than its original release.

Let's look at the position the film holds now, in the twenty-first century. The evolution of the internet has led to a more egalitarian approach to film criticism. These days a film fan is just as likely to refer to a favourite film blogger when looking for a film to watch. If the 1979 audience was dominated by film students and directors, it is now film fans and bloggers who determine the reputation of *Peeping Tom*.

Scorsese makes a powerful point in an interview with Mark Kermode about *Peeping Tom*: 'It speaks directly now, the world we're in, the morbid urge to gaze…YouTube… there's a problem here, cameras in the streets….everybody, we are all being gazed upon. It's like an invasion of who we are as human beings. It's more relevant today than when it came out' (Kermode, 2010).

Many aspects of the film that turned critics against *Peeping Tom* in 1960 have perhaps become less significant. But the central theme of voyeurism – of watching and being observed – is as relevant (and disturbing), if not even more so today than it was in 1960.

Film fan bloggers have continued to write about *Peeping Tom*, regarding it as a lost classic, an intriguing masterpiece. The reappraisal that Scorsese initiated has stuck and *Peeping Tom* is now considered to be a film of significant worth.

I would like to end with what Thelma Schoonmaker says about how Michael Powell continued after *Peeping Tom*.

> He never felt he should not have made the movie. What happened to him afterwards is tragic. But he never stopped dreaming of projects and never became bitter, which is one of the great victories of his life.
>
> Michael had seen many great artists destroyed because they were too far ahead of their time, or couldn't stand studio meddling. Some of the most touching writing in his

autobiography is about Rex Ingram, who taught him how to direct and then crashed and burned because of his battles with Louis B. Mayer. So I think he knew the same thing could happen to him, possibly. Somehow he was able to survive the destruction of his career, and just kept on writing movies he wanted to make but never could. He never lost his enthusiasm for his art. He asked me to put on his gravestone: 'Michael Powell, Film Director and Optimist'. (Unpublished correspondence with the author)

SELECTED BIBLIOGRAPHY

Anon. (1960) as quoted in 'Mr. Michael Powell on Making Horror Films', *The Thunderer*, 5 July.

Ashby, J. & Higson, A. (eds) (2000) *British Cinema, Past and Present*. London: Routledge.

Barr, C. (2005) 'Hitchcock and Powell: Two directions for British cinema', *Screen*, 46.1.

Bloom Walden, K. (2013) *British Film Studios*. Oxford: Shire Publications.

Clover, C. (1992; updated 2015) *Men, Women, and Chain Saws: Gender in the Modern Horror Film (updated edition)*. Princeton: Princeton University Press.

Cooper, I. (2016) *Frightmares: A History of British Horror Cinema*. Leighton Buzzard: Auteur.

Christie, I. & Moor, A. (eds) (2005) *The Cinema of Michael Powell: International Perspectives on an English Film-Maker*. London: British Film Institute.

Cronly, P. (2007) 'Peeping Tom', *The Irish Journal of Gothic and Horror Stories* 3.

Crook, S. (n.d.) 'Peeping Tom: The Myths', powell-pressburger.org

Gallant, C. (2000) *Art of Darkness: The Cinema of Dario Argento*. Guildford: FAB.

Girard, P. (2019) 'The Killing of a Career: The Peeping Tom Scandal', academia.edu https://www.academia.edu/38738648/The_Killing_of_a_Career_The_Peeping_Tom_Scandal

Gottlieb, S. (ed.) (2003) *Alfred Hitchcock: Interviews*. Jackson: University Press of Mississippi.

Gritten, D. (2010) 'Michael Powell's "Peeping Tom": the film that killed a career', *The Telegraph*, 27 August.

Jancovich, M. (1992) *Horror*. London: Batsford.

Jancovich, M. (2002) *Horror, The Film Reader*. London: Routledge.

Johnson, W. (1980) 'Peeping Tom: a second look', *Film Quarterly* Vol. 33, No. 3.

Kelley, B. (1996) 'Michael Powell: Peeping Tom', *Femme Fatale Magazine*, July.

Kermode, M. (2010) Interview with Martin Scorsese conducted on video for *The*

Guardian (November): https://www.theguardian.com/film/video/2010/nov/19/martin-scorsese-mark-kermode-interview

Kristeva, J. (1980) 'Powers of Horror: An Essay in Abjection' reprinted in EUROPEAN PERSPECTIVES: A Series of the Columbia University Press, New York, 1982.

Landy, M. (2014) *British Genres: Cinema and Society, 1930-1960*. Princeton: Princeton University Press.

Lazar, D. (ed.) (2003) *Michael Powell: Interviews*. Jackson: University Press of Mississippi.

Lowenstein, A. (2005) *Shocking Representation: Historical Trauma, National Cinema, and the Modern Horror Film*. New York: Columbia University Press.

MacDonald, K. (1994) *Emeric Pressburger: The Life and Death of a Screenwriter*. London: Faber & Faber.

Massey, A. (2007) *Telling Some Tales*. London: Arrow.

Mulvey, L. (1989) *Visual and Other Pleasures*. Basingstoke: Macmillan: Palgrave.

Powell, D. (1994) 'Peeping Tom review', *The Sunday Times*, June 19.

Powell, M. (1995) *Million Dollar Movie*. London: Random House.

Powell, M. (2000) *A Life in Movies: An Autobiography*. London: Faber & Faber.

Rockoff, A. (2016) *Going to Pieces: The Rise and Fall of the Slasher Film, 1978-1986*. Jefferson: McFarland.

Rossback, N. (n.d.) 'Peeping Tom and the Critical Movie Viewer', academia.edu https://www.academia.edu/30553514/Peeping_Tom_and_the_Critical_Movie_Viewer_pdf

Torok, J-P. (1960) 'Look at the Sea: Peeping Tom', *Positif*, 36.

Truffaut, F. (2017) *Hitchcock*. London: Faber & Faber.

Wood, R. (1983) 'Beauty Bests the Beast', *American Film* 8, p. 63.

WEBSITES

http://www.powell-pressburger.org

https://cinephiliabeyond.org

https://pamela-green.com

http://www.dailyscript.com/scripts/peepingtom.html

https://www.bbfc.co.uk/case-studies/peeping-tom

www.rogerebert.com

Devil's Advocates

"Auteur Publishing's new Devil's Advocates critiques on individual titles offer bracingly fresh perspectives from passionate writers. The series will perfectly complement the BFI archive volumes." Christopher Fowler, Independent on Sunday

The Fly – Emma Westwood

"...an easily digestible read [that] still tells you everything you could ever want to know. The Fly is a film that I love, but still this book found new ways for me to look at it. ...a must read." – Frightfest.co.uk

Frenzy – Ian Cooper

"Repellent and misogynistic or a black comic masterpiece? Like all good film books, it makes you want to watch it again. And again." – Stephen Volk, screenwriter, Gothic, The Awakening, Ghostwatch

The Shining – Laura Mee

"strongly articulated and well-informed... worthwhile reading for anyone interested in the film. ...a focused and provocative argument that does indeed offer a fresh look at a much-analysed but still not exhausted film." – Fantastika Journal

Twin Peaks: Fire Walk With Me – Lindsay Hallam

"Lindsay Hallam does an admirable job of championing FWWM as a film deserving respect and a place in the horror canon. ... a well researched and absorbing work. ... I'd recommend you settle down with some damn fine coffee and cherry pie and give it a read." – FrightFest. co.uk

Printed and bound by CPI Group (UK) Ltd, Croydon, CR0 4YY

25/03/2025

14647349-0001